INTERNATIONAL DEVELOPMENT IN FOCUS

Coping with Climate Change in the Sundarbans

Lessons from Multidisciplinary Studies

SUSMITA DASGUPTA, DAVID WHEELER, MD. ISTIAK SOBHAN,
SUNANDO BANDYOPADHYAY, AINUN NISHAT, AND TAPAS PAUL

Contents

Photos

Tables

Acknowledgments

The authors are grateful to Sumana Bandyopadhyay, Ajanta Dey, Santadas Ghosh, Bansari Guha, Raqubul Hasib, Moqbul Hossain, Mainul Huq, Saiful Islam, Nabendu Sekhar Kar, Zahirul Huque Khan, Chinmoyee Mallik, Dipanwita Mukherjee, Anirban Mukhopadhyay, Md. Golam Mustafa, Subhendu Roy, and Utpal Roy for the underlying research. Special thanks go to Anamitra Anurag Danda, Magda Lovei, Kseniya Lvovsky, Janet Minatelli, Halla Maher Qaddumi, Sanjay Srivastava, and Michael Toman for their advice. Thanks are also extended to Brian Blankespoor, Angie Harney, Roshni Sarah John, Nivedita Moitra, Bridget Rosario, and Elaine Wylie for support of the research. The authors are appreciative of the communications support in posting blogs provided by Shilpa Banerji, Taylor Warren Henshaw, Mohammad Shahedal Kaium, Mehrin Mahbub, Anushka Thewarapperuma, and Julie Ann Vorman. Finally, the authors extend thanks to Pritthijit (Raja) Kundu, Polly Means, and Siobhan Murray for help with the graphics and Norma Adams for editorial support.

About the Authors

Sunando Bandyopadhyay is a professor of geography at the University of Calcutta. His areas of specialization include geomorphology and remote sensing. For the past three decades, he has been actively involved in field-based research on the physical aspects of the lower Ganga–Brahmaputra–Meghna Delta. He has authored two books as well as articles in scientific journals on geomorphic and environmental issues. He has a PhD from the University of Calcutta.

Susmita Dasgupta is a lead environmental economist in the Development Research Group at the World Bank, specializing in environmental management in developing countries. She has conducted extensive analysis on the health hazards of pollution, the poverty-environment nexus, priority setting in pollution control, deforestation, biodiversity loss, the impacts of climate change on coastal zones and climate extremes, climate change adaptation, cost-effective regulations, and monitoring and enforcement of regulations. Her research activities have focused on Bangladesh, Brazil, Cambodia, China, Colombia, Cuba, India, the Islamic Republic of Iran, the Lao People's Democratic Republic, Madagascar, Mexico, Saudi Arabia, Tunisia, Vietnam, and the Republic of Yemen. She has published numerous articles on issues related to development and the environment. She has a PhD from SUNY (State University of New York).

Ainun Nishat is a professor emeritus at the Centre for Climate Change and Environmental Research at BRAC University in Bangladesh. For decades, he has worked as an advocate, educator, and facilitator, championing the wise use of natural resources and sustainable development in Bangladesh. His current research focuses on adaptation to climate change and related policy advocacy. He has a PhD from the University of Strathclyde in the United Kingdom.

Tapas Paul is a lead environmental specialist in the Environment, Natural Resources and Blue Economy Global Practice at the World Bank. In India, he led the World Bank's work on integrated coastal zone management, cleaning of the Ganga River, conservation and development of the Sundarbans, and management of water and natural resources in the Northeast. He also led forestry work in Bangladesh and currently leads fisheries work in the Maldives and India. His work has also focused on countries in Central Asia, East Asia,

Eastern Europe, and Latin America and the Caribbean. His primary research interests and publications focus on green growth, greening regional-level development strategies, and the blue economy. He has a master's degree from the School of Planning and Architecture in New Delhi.

Md. Istiak Sobhan is an environmental specialist in the Environment, Natural Resources and Blue Economy Global Practice at the World Bank. Before joining the World Bank, he worked as a program coordinator at the International Union for Conservation of Nature. His primary research interests and areas of specialization are environmental systems analysis, forestry and biodiversity, and species distribution across the landscape using remote sensing. He has a PhD from Wageningen University in the Netherlands.

David Wheeler is a senior fellow emeritus at the Center for Global Development. In his past role as a lead economist in the World Bank's Development Research Group, he directed a team that worked on environmental policy and research issues in collaboration with policy makers and academics in Africa, Asia, and Latin America. Before joining the World Bank, he taught at the National University of Zaire and Boston University. He has a PhD from MIT (Massachusetts Institute of Technology).

Executive Summary

CLIMATE CHANGE–RELATED THREATS

The Sundarbans—the world's largest contiguous mangrove forest—is internationally recognized for its unique biodiversity and ecological importance (box ES.1). The United Nations Educational, Scientific, and Cultural Organization (UNESCO) declared the Indian and Bangladesh portions of the Sundarbans World Heritage Sites in 1987 and 1997, respectively. The region is also internationally recognized under the Ramsar Convention.

Despite this recognition, including conservation obligations under international conventions and treaties, the Sundarbans is under threat from climate change, along with a combination of natural factors and human actions. The region's land is still changing with the tides, and its rivers are changing their course. Over time, the eastward meandering of the Ganges River is affecting sedimentation and reducing freshwater inflows significantly. In recent decades, human actions—construction of upstream dams, embankments to protect land from tides, overexploitation of mangrove timber, urban and industrial pollution, and mangrove clearing for agriculture and aquaculture—have affected the region's water supplies, sedimentation, topography, and hydrology.

Beyond these concerns, climate-induced changes have significant implications for managing this critical ecosystem and the forest-dependent livelihoods of surrounding inhabitants, which include some of South Asia's poorest and most vulnerable communities. Multifaceted, climate-related threats include sea-level rise, increased atmospheric carbon dioxide (CO_2), higher air and water temperatures, and greater frequency and intensity of precipitation and storms. Climate-induced changes are expected to lead to fragmentation of the Sundarbans landscape, including area loss, progressive water and soil salinization, and changes in flora and fauna. Despite their critical importance, these concerns have not yet been integrated into management protocols for the Sundarbans.

BOX ES.1

The Sundarbans: A wetland of international importance

The Sundarbans is well known for its exceptional diversity of flora and fauna, which features 528 species of vascular plants, 300 species of birds, and 250 fish species. It includes a variety of species of reptiles (58), mammals (42), and amphibians (9); numerous species of insects, crustaceans, invertebrates, and mollusks; and diverse phytoplankton, fungi, bacteria, and zooplankton.

The wetland's ecosystem offers a wide range of vital ecological services. These include carbon sequestration and oxygen production, waste recycling, and trapping of sediment. For millions of people and assets in coastal Bangladesh and West Bengal, the wetland offers cyclone protection and supplies wood for building materials. In addition, it provides a breeding ground and nursery for indigenous and marine fish, which, in turn, may supply food to local populations.

Sources: Danda et al. 2017; Dasgupta et al. 2018; IUCN 2015; Rahman et al. 2015; World Bank 2014.

NEED FOR COMPREHENSIVE DATA AND COLLABORATIVE RESEARCH

The impacts of a changing climate could differ significantly across the Sundarbans when measured in magnitude and time-phasing, leading to differential pressures across the political border for adaptation responses to the same environmental conditions, including when to relocate human communities and endangered species. A review of the literature reveals the scarcity of sound technical knowledge on the impacts of climate change and adaptation measures for the Sundarbans and its inhabitants. Previous studies, which were extremely limited in geographic scope, failed to provide a comprehensive, regional perspective.[1]

To build a knowledge base for sound climate change adaptation and resilience responses, the South Asia Water Initiative (SAWI) has undertaken an analytical program to assess the climate vulnerability of human populations and ecosystems across the Sundarbans landscape. Critical problems addressed include inundation from sea-level rise and cyclone-induced storm surges and salinization of water and soil. The salinization studies highlight implications for the quantity and quality of water resources that are critical for women's and children's health and nutrition.

UNIQUE PROGRAM FEATURES

The analytical program's complex, "out-of-the-box" research design featured (1) a multidisciplinary approach, (2) cross-border research collaboration, and (3) learning from regional and historical perspectives. Numerous cross-cutting, empirical studies were designed and implemented to estimate location-specific, climate vulnerabilities. These multidisciplinary studies were undertaken by a wide array of technical experts, ranging from climate scientists, geographers, GIS specialists, hydrologists, ecologists, and soil scientists to fisheries experts, sociologists, economists, econometricians, engineers, and regional planners.

The program also promoted collaborative research on the Sundarbans between Bangladesh and India, which has been a major challenge since 1947. Technical cooperation involved 17 local researchers from Bangladesh and India.

The research program drew on the complementary skills of Bangladeshi and Indian experts, as well as those of 4 international consultants, who bridged gaps where local expertise was unavailable. Researchers worked together to monitor water quality, design surveys, conduct empirical analyses, and co-author analytic papers. These were used to quantify the vulnerability of both the Sundarbans ecosystem and its poor inhabitants in a changing climate. This included implications for changes in the quality, availability, and productivity of water resources that are critical to women's and children's health and nutrition. To the extent possible, the technical analyses covered the Sundarbans from a regional perspective. However, in cases where Sundarbans data were not uniformly available across both countries, studies were conducted for either the Bangladesh or India segment. Once data are available, the insights drawn and the methodologies established can be extended to or replicated in the other segment.

The research also laid the technical foundation for a better understanding of the physical changes that are driving the responses of human communities and ecosystems. The research team developed historical erosion and accretion records by analyzing pre-1947 maps of the Sundarbans coastline. It compiled and compared data from the Bangladesh and India meteorological departments to develop a combined database of cyclone landfalls along the Sundarbans coastline from 1877 to 2016. It used hydrological models to project the impacts of climate change on salinization in the Bangladesh Sundarbans. These salinization projections were then extrapolated to projections for the Indian Sundarbans, where water-salinity modeling is hindered by data scarcity. The research team also surveyed many local communities to develop analyses of the impacts of environmental degradation on livelihoods, as well as inhabitants' perceptions of climate change risks.

OVERALL LESSONS LEARNED

The overall lesson emerging from this analytical program is that policies for promoting adaptation to climate change are far more effective when informed by area-specific knowledge and analysis. To our knowledge, this is the first cross-boundary study program that has shown how general climate-induced changes in weather patterns, hydrology, and salinity translate to location-specific impacts on coastal communities and ecosystems. Widespread interest in the program has focused particularly on its methodology for identifying the effects on specific resources, livelihoods, and health outcomes. This pragmatic approach to research facilitates the identification of effective, localized policy initiatives to address the increasing impacts of climate change. Although the technical studies focused on the Sundarbans regions of India and Bangladesh, the same methods and modes of analysis could be applied in other coastal areas of the developing world to identify localized climate impacts and potential solutions.

The analytical program's research approach resulted in salient lessons, among which the following are highlighted:

- *History matters.* Setting accurate technical baselines from historical data is an essential prerequisite for understanding the vulnerability of ecosystems and human communities in a changing climate. For example, any assessment of expected area loss of the Sundarbans to sea-level rise must first take into account the geomorphological changes (accretion and erosion) that are taking place over time.

Focus group discussion with women in Mathurapur II, South 24 Parganas

Source: © Susmita Dasgupta / World Bank. Further permission required for reuse.

- *Local knowledge and analysis matter.* With sea-level rise and progressive sali-nization, the developing world's coastal regions will face significant changes in the quality of water and soil, as well as alterations in flora and fauna. It is expected that the lives and livelihoods of poor households, including the regions' most vulnerable population segments (women, children, and the elderly) will be affected the most. But climate impacts and their policy impli-cations will be greatly affected by local socioeconomic, topographical, and environmental conditions. Effective policies must take these local contexts and experiences into account.
- *Local consultation matters.* Localized research cannot identify the key lever-age points for effective policy interventions without understanding the insights, institutions, and incentives of the people who live in the affected areas (photo ES.1).

Contextual lessons: Ecosystem impacts

Climate change has already affected the Sundarbans significantly in terms of sea-level rise (maps ES.1 and ES.2) and resulting salinization of water and soil (figure ES.1). Unless the responsible agencies in both India and Bangladesh are equipped to promote climate resilience, one can expect that future climate-induced changes will undermine regional management.

It is difficult to predict the extent of area loss from sea-level rise in a changing climate without first knowing the region's geomorphological his-tory. Irrespective of climate change, the overall area of the Sundarban islands has been undergoing erosion for quite some time (map ES.1).

MAP ES.1

Sundarbans' accretion and erosion, 1904–24 to 2015–16

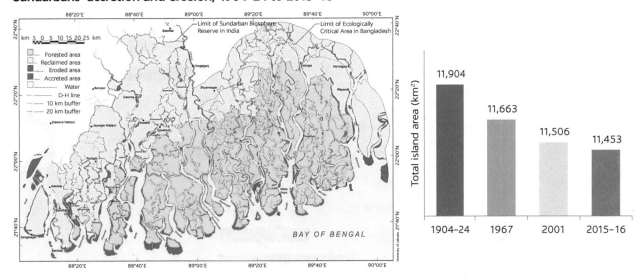

Source: Bandyopadhyay et al. 2018b.
Note: km² = square kilometer.

MAP ES.2

Cyclone landfalls on the Northern Bay of the Bengal Coast, 1877–2016

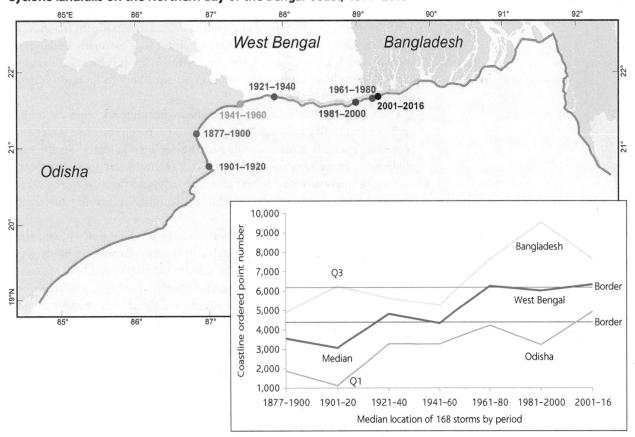

Source: Bandyopadhyay et al. 2018a.
Note: The gradual eastward shift in landfall over the past 56 years toward the West Bengal-Bangladesh border makes the Sundarbans coast (shown in green) highly vulnerable. From 1961 to 2016, storms tended to land in that area. Q = quartile.

FIGURE ES.1

Projected dominance of salt-tolerant mangrove species in the Indian Sundarbans

Net change between 2015 and 2050

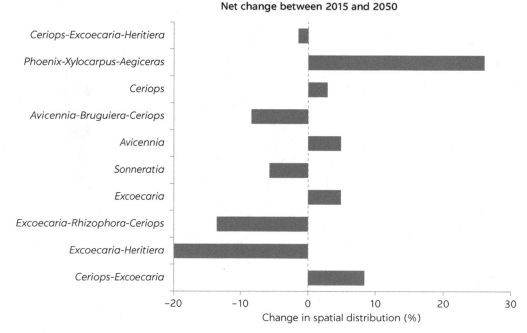

Source: Mukhopadhyay et al. 2019.

With sea-level rise, this trend is expected to lead to significant fragmention of the Sundarbans landscape, causing habitat loss for many endangered species. Landscape fragmentation and wildlife habitat loss (for example, for tigers and venomous snakes), in turn, are likely to increase human-wildlife conflicts in the region.

Currently, the Sundarbans is one of the highest impact zones for tropical cyclones in the Bay of Bengal (map ES.2). As a result, massive losses from recurrent cyclonic storms are one of the region's primary development challenges. In a changing climate, a rising sea level and increased ocean-surface temperature can be expected to further intensify storm surges. Planning for cyclone resilience is thus critical for the region's sustainable development.

With sea-level rise, progressive salinization of water and soil and alterations in flora and fauna are inevitable in the Sundarbans. In many areas, water salinity will reach near-ocean salinity (32 parts per 1,000, or ppt) by 2050, which is likely to cause serious freshwater shortages. The core forest and nearby populated areas can expect to see significant changes in mangrove composition and coastal aquatic ecosystems, with salt-tolerant species (for example, *Avicennia*, *Bruguiera*, *Excoecaria*, and *Ceriops*) dominating the landscape (figure ES.1).

Contextual lessons: Population impacts

With sea-level rise and progressive salinization, changes in the quality of water and soil, as well as alterations in flora and fauna, will significantly affect the lives and livelihoods of poor households, including the region's most vulnerable population segments (that is, women, children, and the elderly).

Shortage of drinking water due to the salinization of rivers and groundwater will have significant implications for the time-activity patterns of households, especially during the dry season (table ES.1). Women will be affected disproportionately since more of their time is spent accesssing potable water. As the salinity of drinking water increases, the expected adverse impacts on human health include dehydration, hypertension, prenatal complications, and increased infant mortality.

Scarcity of water for dry-season agriculture, decline in freshwater fish species, and changes in the composition of mangrove species resulting from progressive salinization will adversely impact the natural resource–based livelihoods of poor households in the region (for example, fishers relying on freshwater capture species).

With rising river salinity, the probable decline in wild (indigenous) freshwater fish species will have significant implications for the nutrition of the rural poor (figure ES.2). These species are the major dietary source of animal protein, minerals, and essential micronutrients for poor and extremely poor populations in the region. The stakes are particularly high for mother-child health, given that chronic and acute malnutrition levels in the region are higher than the World Health Organization's thresholds for public-health emergencies, as indicated by statistics on child wasting and stunting and anemia among women of reproductive age.

Varying patterns of floods and droughts with climate change will also affect mother-child health through their impacts on the price and availability of critical nutrients (for example, fish and other animal-source food), environmental conditions, and family hygiene.

TABLE ES.1 **Field measurements of water salinity in the Indian Sundarbans**

SALINITY (ppt)	MINIMUM	MAXIMUM	MEAN	MEDIAN
Water tube well and water taps (sampled from different villages)	0.41	2.66	0.87	0.84
Water from rivers (sampled at locations nearest the villages)	13	27	21.94	22.55

Source: Adapted from Dasgupta, Ghosh, and Wheeler 2020.
Note: Water is not potable if salinity exceeds 1 part per 1,000 (ppt).

FIGURE ES.2

Predicted losses of freshwater fish habitats in poor areas, 2012–50

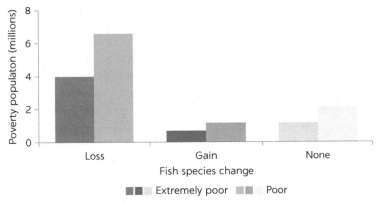

Source: Adapted from Dasgupta et al. 2017.
Note: In areas with poor populations, the prevalence of species loss is six times greater than species gain.

MAP ES.3

Disproportionate exposure of Bangladesh's coastal poor to water salinity and storm surges

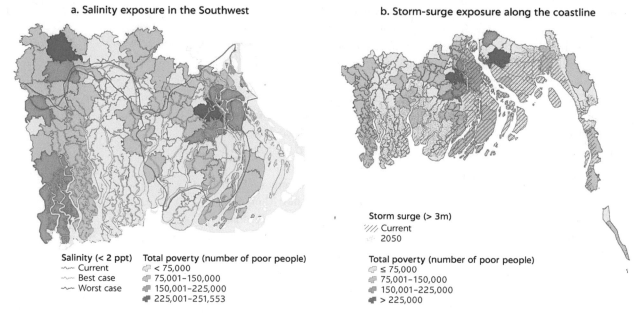

a. Salinity exposure in the Southwest

b. Storm-surge exposure along the coastline

Salinity (< 2 ppt)
- Current
- Best case
- Worst case

Total poverty (number of poor people)
- < 75,000
- 75,001–150,000
- 150,001–225,000
- 225,001–251,553

Storm surge (> 3m)
- Current
- 2050

Total poverty (number of poor people)
- ≤ 75,000
- 75,001–150,000
- 150,001–225,000
- > 225,000

Source: Dasgupta 2015.
Note: m = meter; ppt = parts per 1,000.

Poor households in the region are disadvantaged by the lack of access to land. Many end up settling in low-lying areas close to the coast and creeks. This, in turn, puts their livelihoods at risk from cyclones, tidal inundation, and salinization. With climate change, the increasing frequency of cyclone strikes and intensity, greater risk of inundation, and progressive salinization mean that the poorest households will be the most vulnerable (map ES.3). Yet they will be the last to flee since high land prices and a lack of employment opportunities elsewhere will restrict their options as the sea moves steadily inland.

COPING WITH VULNERABILITY

Proactive adaptation to reduce the vulnerability of the Sundarbans to climate change is essential for "climate-smart" sustainable development and poverty reduction in the region. Cost-effective adaptation to climate-related changes in the Sundarbans will require increased public investment. It will also depend on local support for appropriate collective action. Perceptions of environmental problems vary significantly both across and within localities. Thus, locally oriented collective action, along with local governance that promotes nonelite participation, is needed for effective management of environmental resources in the Sundarbans.

Mangrove protection and restoration are urgently needed to reduce the damage to adjacent coastal lands from cyclonic storm surges. However, the protective capacity of mangroves varies, depending on the tree species, forest width, and planting density. Among the species commonly found in the Sundarbans, *Sonneratia apetala* causes maximum obstruction to surge water, followed by *Avicennia officinalis* and *Heritiera fomes*.

Reduction in surge height from mangrove afforestation

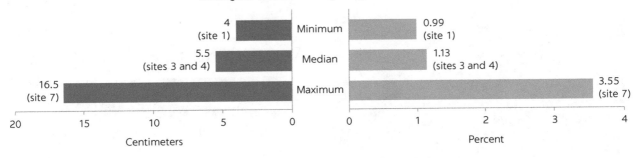

a. Range of attenuated surge height from baseline

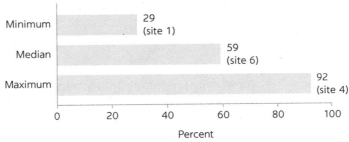

b. Range of change in water-flow velocity

Source: Dasgupta et al. 2019.
Note: This study evaluated the protective capacity of five commonly found mangrove species at seven sites in Bangladesh where surge heights can reach up to 4 meters.

In the densely populated, cyclone-prone reclaimed areas of the Sundarbans, where surge heights can reach 1.5–4.0 meters, protecting against inundation risk requires mangrove protection and restoration ("green" infrastructure) in combination with strengthening built ("gray") infrastructure, such as cyclone shelters and embankments. By significantly reducing water-flow velocity, healthy mangroves protect the built infrastructure from breaching, toe erosion, and other types of damage, thereby contributing to significant savings in rehabilitation and maintenance costs (figure ES.3). This means that healthy mangroves offer "win-win" adaptation measures since they also enhance livelihood opportunities.

Field investigations identified numerous adaptation measures for reducing the exposure of vulnerable populations to cyclone disasters. Among others, they include training the out-migrating working-age population, enhancing eco-friendly livelihood options for the remaining population, and developing infrastructure strategies as protection from salinization.

As noted above, adaptation measures to reduce cyclone exposure should include a combination of "green" (mangrove) and "gray" (built) infrastructure (photo ES.2). In addition to embankments and public cyclone shelters, gray-infrastructure options include the presence of brick houses on stilts in every neighborhood, which function as shelters of last resort. Another critical element is improvement in small-area early-warning and disaster-forecasting systems.

Additional infrastructure investment is needed to protect from growing salinization. The main options include assistance with small-scale, local desalinization plants; rainwater harvesting; and precautionary measures taken before constructing buildings, roads, and other built-infrastructure.

PHOTO ES.2

Limiting cyclone exposure with green and gray infrastructure

Sources: © Pritthijit (Raja) Kundu (left); © Md. Istiak Sobhan / World Bank (right). Reproduced with permission; further permission required for reuse.

For working-age people pursuing voluntary out-migration, training and skills development are needed to help strengthen their human-capital and earning potential. The government should persuade designated training institutes to put forward training programs in climate-vulnerable areas and provide eligible local people with redeemable coupons that can only be used for those training programs. Suggested areas of training include commercial driving for men, textile-factory work for women, construction work, and cleaning and food-sector services (for foreign employment), along with job-placement services and provision of loans for financing relocation.

Support in the form of microenterprise start-up financing or training is also needed to assist the nonmigrating population in pursuing or enhancing eco-friendly livelihoods (for example, sunflower cultivation, mud-crab culture, homestead pond aquaculture, community-based fisheries management, commercial apiculture, and nature-based tourism).

WILLINGNESS FOR COLLABORATIVE RESEARCH AND MANAGEMENT

During the collaborative design and implementation of the program studies, it became clear that technical experts in both Bangladesh and India are willing and available to work together on managing the transboundary Sundarbans biosphere. Successful resilience planning between the two neighboring countries requires a collaborative work arrangement that draws on their complementary skills. Working together is both feasible and effective for establishing a common understanding of shared challenges and a respectful discussion space in which to carry out resilience planning.

A highlight of the research collaboration between Bangladesh and India was a knowledge exchange workshop on vulnerability of the Sundarbans in a changing climate, held in Calcutta in February 2017 and attended by 400 researchers from both countries. The second day of the workshop included a hands-on training session, in which Bangladeshi experts shared their experience on modeling of storm surge and salinity intrusion with their Indian counterparts. This knowledge exchange sparked a memorandum of understanding

(MoU) for collaborative research between Calcutta University and Khulna University, and joint study tours are under way.

KNOWLEDGE SHARING BEYOND THE STUDY REGION

Worldwide, some 600 million people currently live in low-elevation coastal zones that will be affected by progressive salinization and inundation with sea-level rise in a changing climate. Recently published scientific reports suggest that sea level may rise by 1 meter or more in the 21st century, which would increase the vulnerable population to about 1 billion. Families in the Sundarbans region are already on the front line of climate change. Their experience, behavior, and adaptation signal future decisions by hundreds of millions of families that will face similar threats by 2100. Thus, the opportunities for knowledge sharing between countries that feature low-lying deltaic areas are significant.

The methodologies and findings of these studies have been presented at several professional conferences and various universities and research organizations across South Asia and East Asia, as well as to a number of the World Bank's development partners and policy makers in its client countries. From the interest expressed during these presentations, it is clear that significant opportunities are available for knowledge sharing and information exchange between countries in the Bengal and Mekong deltas, many of which are facing similar challenges in a changing climate (photo ES.3). Various countries have already expressed interest in learning from each others' successes and failures. The World Bank's convening capacity as a knowledge bank can facilitate this process.

PHOTO ES.3

Sharing learning from the analytic program with the Lower Mekong Public Policy Initiative

Source: © Pritthijit (Raja) Kundu. Reproduced with permission from Pritthijit (Raja) Kundu; further permission required for reuse.
Note: The event took place in Ho Chi Minh City, Vietnam, on December 9, 2016.

NOTE

1. Previous studies were often restricted to a few blocks or *mouzas* (administrative districts corresponding to specific land areas with one or more settlements).

REFERENCES

Bandyopadhyay, S., S. Dasgupta, Z. H. Khan, and D. Wheeler. 2018a. "Cyclonic Storm Landfalls in Bangladesh, West Bengal and Odisha, 1877–2016: A Spatiotemporal Analysis." Policy Research Working Paper 8316, World Bank, Washington, DC.

Bandyopadhyay, S., N. S. Kar, S. Dasgupta, and D. Mukherjee. 2018b. "Long-Term Island Area Alternations in the India and Bangladeshi Sundarban: An Assessment Using Cartographic and Remote Sending Sources." Paper prepared for the Sundarbans Targeted Environmental Studies, South Asia Water Initiative, World Bank, Washington, DC.

Danda, A. A., A. K. Joshi, A. Ghosh, and R. Saha, eds. 2017. "State of Art Report on Biodiversity in Indian Sundarbans." World Wide Fund for Nature–India, New Delhi.

Dasgupta, S. 2015. "Left Unattended 5.3 Million of Bangladesh's Poor Will Be Vulnerable to the Effects of Climate Change in 2050." *Let's Talk Development* (blog), April 6. World Bank, Washington, DC. blogs.worldbank.org/developmenttalk/left-unattended-53 -million-bangladesh-s-poor-will-be-vulnerable-effects-climate-change-2050.

Dasgupta, S., S. Ghosh, and D. Wheeler. 2020. "Drinking Water Salinity in Indian Sundarban" (blog). World Bank, Washington, DC. http://www.sundarbansonline.org/wp -content/uploads/2020/03/Note-Drinking-Water-Salinity-in-Indian-Sundarban.pdf.

Dasgupta, S., M. Huq, M. G. Mustafa, M. I. Sobhan, and D. Wheeler. 2017. "The Impact of Aquatic Salinization on Fish Habitats and Poor Communities in a Changing Climate: Evidence from Southwest Coastal Bangladesh." *Ecological Economics* 139 (2017): 128–39.

Dasgupta, S., M. Huq, I. Sobhan, and D. Wheeler. 2018. "Sea-Level Rise and Species Conservation in Bangladesh's Sundarbans Region." *Journal of Management and Sustainability* 8 (1): 1–12.

Dasgupta, S., M. S. Islam, M. Huq, Z. H. Khan, and M. R. Hasib. 2019. "Quantifying the Protective Capacity of Mangroves from Storm Surges in Coastal Bangladesh." *PLoS One* 14 (3): e0214079. http://doi.org/10.1371/journalpone.0214079.

IUCN (International Union for Conservation of Nature). 2015. *Red List of Bangladesh: A Brief on Assessment Result 2015*, 24. Dhaka: IUCN.

Mukhopadhyay, A., D. Wheeler, S. Dasgupta, A. Dey, and I. Sobhan. 2019. "Mangrove Spatial Distribution in the Indian Sundarbans: Predicting Salinity-Induced Migration." *Journal of Management and Sustainability* 9(1).

Rahman, M. S., M. H. Gazi, S. A. Khan, and N. U. Sarder. 2015. "An Annotated Checklist of the Vascular Plants of Sundarban Mangrove Forest of Bangladesh." *Bangladesh Journal of Plant Taxonomy* 22 (1): 17–41.

World Bank. 2014. *Building Resilience for Sustainable Development of the Sundarbans: Strategy Report*. No. 88061-IN. South Asia Region, Sustainable Development Department, Environment and Water Resources Management Unit. Washington, DC: World Bank.

Abbreviations

BMD	Bangladesh Meteorological Department
cm	centimeter
FAO	Food and Agriculture Organization
GHG	greenhouse gas
GIS	geographic information system
IBTrACS	International Best Track Archive for Climate Stewardship
IMD	India Meteorological Department
IUCN	International Union for Conservation of Nature
IWM	Institute of Water Modelling
km^2	square kilometer
m	meter
mm	millimeter
NEWS	Nature Environment and Wildlife Society
NFHS	National Family Health Survey
PPL	prawn postlarvae
ppt	parts per 1,000
SAWI	South Asia Water Initiative
WHO	World Health Organization

1 Introduction

CONTEXT

The Sundarbans is the world's largest remaining contiguous mangrove forest,[1,2] straddling large portions of coastal Bangladesh and India. The region encompasses a total area of 10,200 km², approximately 60 percent (about 6,000 km²) of which lies within the boundaries of Bangladesh and the rest (about 4,200 km²) in West Bengal (India). This internationally important wetland is known for its exceptional biodiversity (photo 1.1). This includes 528 species of vascular plants (Rahman et al. 2015); 42 mammals; 300 birds; 58 reptiles; 9 amphibians; 250 fish; numerous species of insects, crustaceans, invertebrates, and mollusks; and diverse phytoplankton, fungi, bacteria and zooplankton (Danda et al. 2017; IUCN 2015).[3] In 1875, before the partition of India, the Sundarbans was declared a reserve forest. The United Nations Educational, Scientific, and Cultural Organization (UNESCO) declared the Indian and Bangladesh portions World Heritage Sites in 1987 and 1997, respectively. The region is also internationally recognized under the Ramsar Convention. In addition, the Sundarbans is home to some of South Asia's poorest and most vulnerable communities (O'Donnell and Wodon 2015; World Bank 2014).

The Sundarbans ecosystem offers a wide range of vital ecological services. These include: (1) trapping sediment and land formation; (2) cyclone protection for millions of people and assets in coastal Bangladesh and West Bengal; (3) providing a breeding ground and nursery for indigenous and marine fish, as well as other aquatic life; (4) wood production; (5) providing food and building materials; (6) oxygen production; (7) waste recycling; and (8) carbon sequestration (Dasgupta et al. 2018; World Bank 2014).

Despite recognition of its unique biodiversity and ecological importance—including obligations for its conservation under international conventions and treaties—the Sundarbans is currently threatened by a combination of natural factors and human actions. Its land is still changing with the tides, and its rivers are changing their course. Over time, the eastward meandering of the Ganges River is affecting sedimentation and reducing freshwater inflows significantly. In addition to natural factors, human actions—construction of upstream dams, embankments to protect land from tides, overexploitation of mangrove timber, urban and industrial pollution, and mangrove clearing for agriculture and

PHOTO 1.1

The Sundarbans: Tidal-wetland forest delta

- Sundarbans is the largest remaining contiguous mangrove forest in the world.

- Sundarbans is a unique ecosystem and rich wildlife habitat.
  - 350 plant species
  - 250 fish species
  - 300 bird species
  - 42 mammals
  - 58 reptiles

- Sundarbans is a wetland of international importance:
  - Ramsar site
  - UNESCO World Heritage site

Sundarbans is home to some of the poorest and most vulnerable communities in South Asia.

Sources: © Pritthijit (Raja) Kundu (top and middle left); © Ajanta Dey (bottom left); © iStockphoto.com / Jamen Percy (right). Used with permission; further permission required for reuse.
Note: Area: 10,200 km² straddling portions of Bangladesh and India. km² = square kilometer.

aquaculture—have all affected the region's water supplies, sedimentation, topography, and hydrology. Human-induced losses at the local level will probably continue, with climate change likely to aggravate current problems (Raha et al. 2013; World Bank 2014).

On top of other natural factors and human actions, climate change poses major threats to the Sundarbans; but these have not yet been integrated into regional management protocols (Agrawala et al. 2003; O'Donnell and Wodon 2015). Climate change–related threats include sea-level rise, rise in atmospheric carbon dioxide (CO_2), increased air and water temperature, changes in the frequency and intensity of precipitation and storms, and salinization of water and soil (Alongi 2008; Dasgupta et al. 2016). Climate-induced changes are expected to lead to fragmentation of the landscape, including area loss, progressive water and soil salinization, and changes in flora and fauna. The implications of these changes for current and future management of this critical ecosystem and the forest-dependent livelihoods of its inhabitants are significant (Islam and Gnauck 2007; O'Donnell and Wodon 2015). A review of the literature reveals the scarcity of sound technical knowledge on the impacts of climate change and adaptation measures for the Sundarbans and its inhabitants. Previous studies were extremely limited in geographic scope, often restricted to a few *mouzas* or blocks, thus failing to provide a comprehensive regional perspective.[4]

PROGRAM OBJECTIVE AND ACTIVITIES

To bridge this knowledge gap, the analytical program, Sundarbans Targeted Environmental Studies, was funded by the South Asia Water Initiative (SAWI) under the Sundarbans Focus Area.[5] Several hydrological, ecological, and

PHOTO 1.2
Technical studies conducted under the analytical program

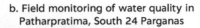

a. Household survey in Gosaba,
South 24 Paraganas

b. Field monitoring of water quality in
Patharpratima, South 24 Parganas

Source: © Santadas Ghosh. Reproduced with permission from Santadas Ghosh; further permission required for reuse.

econometric studies were undertaken to assess the vulnerability of the biodiversity and population of the Sundarbans in a changing climate, as well as identify appropriate adaptation measures. The expectation was that this initiative would enhance awareness about climate change risks, promote technical cooperation between Bangladesh and India, build the knowledge base to support joint management, and facilitate planning a holistic approach to the sustainable management of this extremely fragile mangrove forest.

The technical studies undertaken established research collaboration between Bangladesh and India, drawing on the complementary skills of Bangladeshi and Indian experts (photo 1.2). Multidisciplinary researchers (for example, ecologists, economists, engineers, fishery experts, geographers, geographic information system [GIS] specialists, hydrologists, remote-sensing specialists, and sociologists) from the two neighboring countries worked with international econometricians and GIS specialists to design and conduct the studies (appendix A).

Researchers from the two countries worked together to design surveys, conduct empirical analyses, and co-author analytic papers to quantify (1) the vulnerability of the Sundarbans ecosystem in a changing climate and (2) the vulnerability of the Sundarbans' poor inhabitants in a changing climate, including implications for changes in the quality, availability, and productivity of water resources that are critical for women's and children's health and nutrition.[6] The researchers then worked together to identify adaptation measures to address the vulnerability of the Sundarbans and its inhabitants. The process facilitated large-scale knowledge exchange between the two countries, which has been a major challenge since the partition of India in 1947.

To the extent possible, the technical analysis covered the Sundarbans from a regional perspective; however, one should note that data are not uniformly available across the Bangladesh and Indian Sundarbans. To conduct comprehensive, location-specific vulnerability assessments, these studies compiled information from all open-access secondary sources, complemented by primary data

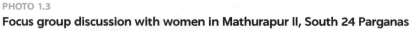

PHOTO 1.3

Focus group discussion with women in Mathurapur II, South 24 Parganas

Source: © Susmita Dasgupta / World Bank. Further permission required for reuse.

collected from field surveys and measurements (photo 1.3). When data scarcity prevented comprehensive analysis, studies were conducted with currently available data for the Bangladesh or Indian Sundarbans. These studies were peer-reviewed, and methods that can be applied to the other segment of the Sundarbans (on the availability of future data) were established. Overall, the analytical program compiled 3 geocoded data sets and produced 16 technical reports and journal articles, as well as 10 published web feature stories.[7]

THIS BOOK'S PURPOSE AND ORGANIZATION

This book summarizes the main findings from the technical reports produced by these multidisciplinary studies. These include the expected impacts of sea-level rise on the Sundarbans in a changing climate; implications for the region's poor, particularly the most vulnerable segments of its population; and recommended adaptation measures, based on the results of technical studies, focus group discussions, and field surveys.

The book is organized in six chapters. Chapter 2 reviews the current climate challenges that the Sundarbans ecosystem is already experiencing and, using these baseline results, identifies threats from further fragmentation of the landscape and progressive salinization of rivers to the region's flora and fauna in a changing climate. Chapter 3 considers how changes to the natural-resource base from progressive salinization are affecting mother-child health, as well as the livelihoods of poor households. Chapter 4 identifies adaptation measures to reduce local people's exposure to storm-surge risk, promote eco-friendly livelihood options, and protect physical assets from salinity-induced impacts. Chapter 5 summarizes the lessons learned, including those that are especially significant for World Bank operations. Chapter 6 describes the collaborative process through which the initiative has strengthened the institutional capacity of Bangladesh and India to jointly manage the Sundarbans region, which lays the foundation for comparative-policy research in the region and other coastal countries facing similar problems. Chapter 7 concludes.

NOTES

1. The term *mangrove* has been defined as a "tree, shrub, palm, or ground fern, generally exceeding more than half a meter in height [that] normally grows above mean sea level in the intertidal zones of marine coastal environments or estuarine margins" (Duke 1992). The mangrove ecosystem represents an inter-phase between terrestrial and marine communities, which receive a daily input of water from the ocean (tides) and freshwater, sediments, nutrients, and silt deposits from upland rivers. Mangroves may grow as trees or shrubs according to the climate, salinity of water, topography, and edaphic features of the area in which they exist.
2. The second-largest contiguous mangrove forest in the world is only about one-10th the size of the Sundarbans.
3. According to the latest (2015) accounting by the International Union for Conservation of Nature (IUCN), 19 birds, 11 mammals, and 1 reptile in the Sundarbans are already regionally extinct (IUCN 2015).
4. The term *mouza* refers to a type of administrative district corresponding to a specific land area with one or more settlements.
5. The Sundarbans Focus Area of the South Asia Water Initiative (SAWI) aimed to enhance bilateral and technical cooperation between Bangladesh and India to support operationalization of the Sundarbans agreements and joint water-resources management in the Sundarbans.
6. International consultants were engaged only to bridge the skills gap when local expertise was unavailable.
7. The electronic version of this book includes embedded hyperlinks to the data sets, technical reports and journal articles, and web feature stories, organized by chapter theme (see annexes 2A, 3A, and 4A).

REFERENCES

Agrawala, S., T. Ota, A. U. Ahmed, J. Smith, and M. van Aalst. 2003. *Development and Climate Change in Bangladesh: Focus on Coastal Flooding and the Sundarbans.* Paris: Organisation for Economic Co-operation and Development.

Alongi, D. M. 2008. "Mangrove Forests: Resilience, Protection from Tsunamis, and Responses to Global Climate Change." *Estuarine, Coastal and Shelf Science* 76 (1): 1–13.

Danda, A.A., Joshi, A.K., Ghosh, A. and Saha, R., eds. 2017. "State of Art Report on Biodiversity in Indian Sundarbans." World Wide Fund for Nature-India, New Delhi.

Dasgupta, S., M. Hossain, M. Huq, and D. Wheeler. 2016. "Facing the Hungry Tide: Climate Change, Livelihood Threats and Household Responses in Coastal Bangladesh." *Climate Change Economics* 7 (3): 1–25.

Dasgupta, S., M. Huq, I. Sobhan, and D. Wheeler. 2018. "Sea-Level Rise and Species Conservation in Bangladesh's Sundarbans Region." *Journal of Management and Sustainability* 8 (1): 1–12.

Duke, N.C. 1992. "Mangrove Floristics and Biogeography." In *Tropical Mangrove Ecosystems*, edited by A. I. Robertson and D. M. Alongi, 63–100. Washington, DC: American Geophysical Union.

Islam, S. N., and A. Gnauck. 2007. "Effects of Salinity Intrusion in the Mangroves Wetlands Ecosystems in Sunderbans: An Alternative Approach for Sustainable Management." In *Wetlands: Monitoring, Modelling and Management*, edited by Tomasz Okruszko, Edward Maltby, Jan Szatylowicz, Dorota Miroslaw-Swiatek, and Wiktor Kotowski. London: Taylor and Francis Group.

IUCN (International Union for Conservation of Nature). 2015. *Red List of Bangladesh: A Brief on Assessment Result 2015*, 24. Dhaka: IUCN.

O'Donnell, A., and Q. Wodon, eds. 2015. *Climate Change Adaptation and Social Resilience in the Sundarbans*. London: Routledge.

Raha, A. K., S. Zaman, K. Sengupta, S. B. Bhattacharyya, S. Raha, K. Banerjee, and A. Mitra. 2013. "Climate Change and Sustainable Livelihood Programme: A Case Study from Indian Sundarbans." *Journal of Ecology* 107 (64): 335–48.

Rahman, M. S., M. H. Gazi, S. A. Khan, and N. U. Sarder. 2015. "An Annotated Checklist of the Vascular Plants of Sundarban Mangrove Forest of Bangladesh." *Bangladesh Journal of Plant Taxonomy* 22 (1): 17–41.

World Bank. 2014. *Building Resilience for Sustainable Development of the Sundarbans: Strategy Report*. No. 88061-IN. South Asia Region, Sustainable Development Department, Environment and Water Resources Management Unit. Washington, DC: World Bank.

2 Vulnerability of the Sundarbans Ecosystem

INTRODUCTION

Worldwide, sea-level rise has been identified as the greatest climate change–related threat to mangrove forests, including the Sundarbans (Field 1995; McLeod and Salm 2006; Nicholls, Hoozemans, and Marchand 1999). With virtual certainty that sea-level rise will continue beyond 2100 even if greenhouse gas (GHG) emissions are stabilized today, how vulnerable is the Sundarbans to inundation and area loss from sea-level rise and cyclone-induced storm surges, as well as water and soil salinization and the resulting degradation of natural resources? How are the poorest, forest-dependent families in the region affected? To answer these questions, this analytical program addressed the technical-knowledge gap on the expected impacts of sea-level rise on the Sundarbans ecosystem and its inhabitants in a changing climate. The first step was to compile or construct three open-access, geocoded data sets to identify challenges that the region faces in the current climate (annex 2A). These data sets provided the baseline for conducting location-specific vulnerability assessments in a changing climate, the results of which are reported in six technical reports and journal articles (annex 2A).

SETTING THE BASELINE: THE SUNDARBANS IN THE CURRENT CLIMATE

To better grasp the challenges that the Sundarbans faces in a changing climate, the analytical program began by compiling geocoded historical data for the entire landscape spanning Bangladesh and India. Starting with a historic perspective was necessary in order to understand the region's current conditions, including identifying any climate challenges it is already experiencing. This information on current conditions also served as a baseline for conducting location-specific vulnerability assessments in a changing climate.

Area loss

Any assessment of the likely loss of area in this iconic landscape due to sea-level rise must first take into account the geomorphological changes that are currently taking place in the coastal areas (Allison 1998). The Sundarbans is located in the tidally active Ganga-Brahmaputra Delta, which is still undergoing erosion and accretion (Allison and Kepple 2001; Bandyopadhyay 2019) (photo 2.1). Therefore, understanding the region's geology is a prerequisite for attempting any technical analysis of its vulnerability to sea-level rise (Rahman, Dragoni, and El-Marri 2011). A major accomplishment unique to this analytical program was its ability to address the issue of area change in a systematic pattern, using archived maps in India that predate the 1947 partition.

To assess the risk of permanent inundation of land areas in the Sundarbans from sea-level rise, the researchers first constructed a data set from a mosaic of Survey of India "inch" topographical maps (1904–24), Corona space photos (1967), IRS-1D L3+Pan (2001), and IRS-R2 L4-mx (2015–16) satellite images in order to understand the erosion and accretion of the region over time. Analysis of the newly constructed data set indicates that the overall Sundarban-islands area has been undergoing a linear erosional trend; in 1904–24, the total island area was 11,904 km², which fell to 11,663 km² by 1967, falling further to 11,506 km² in 2001 and 11,453 km² by 2015–16 (map 2.1). This declining trend holds true whether the Indian and Bangladesh portions of the Sundarbans are considered separately or grouped together.

Comparison of the various images highlights the extent of erosion along nearly the entire surface of the delta and accretion in the interior parts, mainly in the west. The rate of linear retreat of coastlines is as high as 40 m per year for some of the islands, which will face complete obliteration within the next 50–100 years. The southern, exterior localities are erosion-prone since they are vulnerable to storm waves and, because of abandonment of the deltaic distributaries feeding the western Sundarbans portion of the Ganga-Brahmaputra Delta, are not being replenished by up-country sediments. In contrast, many of the northern interior islands have registered

PHOTO 2.1

Coastal erosion in Sagar, South 24 Parganas

Source: © Sunando Bandyopadhyay. Reproduced with permission from Sunando Bandyopadhyay; further permission required for reuse.

MAP 2.1

Sundarbans' accretion and erosion, 1904–24 to 2015–16

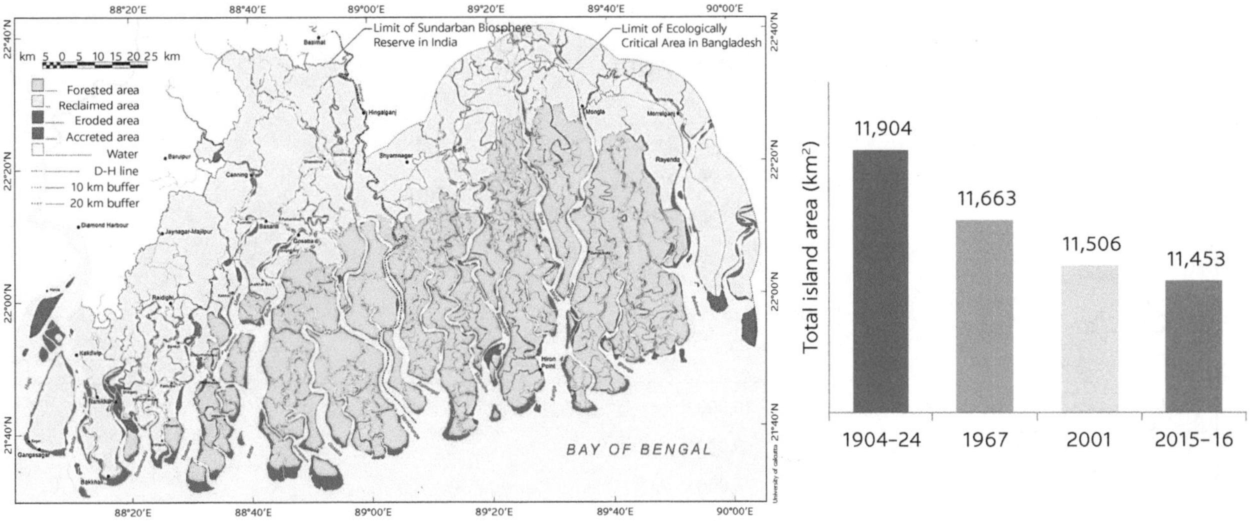

Source: Bandyopadhyay et al. 2018b.
Note: km² = square kilometer.

accretion as the creeks silt up, and two or more islands have coalesced from larger islands.[1] These geomorphological changes are taking place irrespective of climate change.

Tropical storms and cyclones

Tropical storms and cyclones are some of the world's most forceful and destructive weather systems. During the passage of a single tropical cyclone, the loss and damage inflicted by a few hours' battering by waves, winds, and surges can undo the gains from many years of accumulative processes.[2] Historically, tropical storms have accounted for the greatest threat to the Sundarbans, owing to the region's proximity to the Bay of Bengal (Chaudhuri and Chattopadhyay 2004).[3] With climate change, it is feared that an increase in ocean surface temperature and sea-level rise will intensify storm surges (Deo and Garner 2014). It is thus critical to gain a deeper understanding of the patterns of cyclonic storm landfall for management of the Sundarbans, particularly since massive losses from recurrent cyclonic storms are one of the region's primary development challenges.

To understand the long-term trends of cyclonic storm landfalls in the region, this study constructed a georeferenced panel database of cyclonic storm tracks, landfall locations, and impact zones in Bangladesh, West Bengal, and Odisha between 1877 and 2016 from the Bangladesh Meteorological Department (BMD), India Meteorological Department (IMD), and the IBTrACS database maintained by the Global Data Center for Meteorology and operated by the US National Oceanic and Atmospheric Administration. Data were analyzed for 168 cyclone strikes along the 1,259 km impact zone in Bangladesh, West Bengal, and Odisha over seven historical periods: 1877–1900, 1901–20, 1921–40, 1941–60, 1961–80, 1981–2000, and 2001–16. The results revealed that, despite pronounced period-to-period shifts, the median location of cyclones has shifted eastward over time, with the highest-impact zones currently found in northern Odisha and the Sundarbans region of West Bengal (map 2.2).[4]

MAP 2.2

Cyclone landfalls on the Northern Bay of the Bengal Coast, 1877–2016

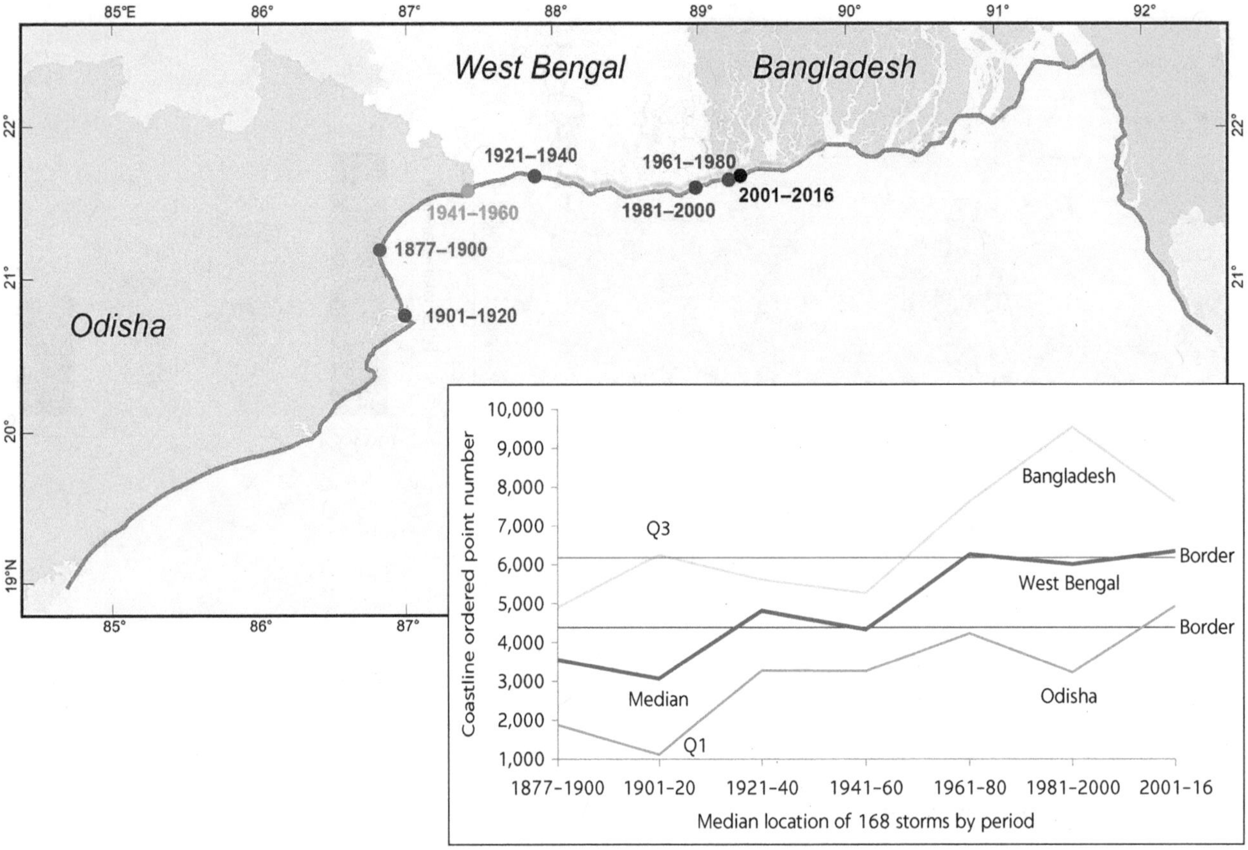

Source: Bandyopadhyay et al. 2018a.
Note: The gradual eastward shift in landfall over the past 56 years toward the West Bengal-Bangladesh border makes the Sundarbans coast (shown in green) highly vulnerable. From 1961 to 2016, storms tended to make landfall in that area. Q = quartile.

Water salinity

Understanding current and future water (and soil) salinity are critical for management of the Sundarbans. as it is feared that climate-induced changes in sea level, temperature, and rainfall, along with altered riverine flows from the Himalayas due to gradual eastward meandering of the Ganges River, will spread and further intensify salinization of surface water and soil in the region by 2050 (Akhter, Hasan, and Khan 2012; IWM 2005; Mohal, Khan, and Rahman 2006; United Kingdom, Department of Environment, Food and Rural Affairs 2007). High water salinity is already a serious problem in the Sundarbans during the dry season and following cyclones (Petersen and Shireen 2001). Anecdotal evidence indicates surface-water salinity increases steadily from October to May of each year.

In Bangladesh, the Institute of Water Modelling (IWM) regularly monitors river-water salinity in the country's southwest coastal region, which includes the Bangladesh Sundarbans; however, water monitoring in the Indian Sundarbans is sparse. In the absence of a geocoded database on water salinity for the Indian Sundarbans, this analytical program generated a baseline profile, later complemented by primary field measurements. The baseline profile was

PHOTO 2.2
Water salinity monitoring in Gosaba, South 24 Parganas

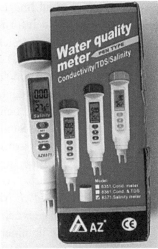

Source: © Santadas Ghosh (left). Reproduced with permission from Santadas Ghosh; further permission required for reuse.

TABLE 2.1 **Field measurements of water salinity in the Indian Sundarbans**

SALINITY (ppt)	MINIMUM	MAXIMUM	MEAN	MEDIAN
Water tube well or water taps (sampled from different villages)	0.41	2.66	0.87	0.84
Water from rivers (sampled at locations nearest the villages)	13	27	21.94	22.55

Source: Adapted from Dasgupta, Ghosh, and Wheeler 2020.
Note: Water is not potable if salinity exceeds 1 part per 1,000 (ppt).

created using a high-resolution, spatial point file from field measurements covering 4 years (2012–15) taken by the Nature Environment and Wildlife Society (NEWS) and World Wildlife Fund–India (WWF-India). The researchers collected water samples from the Bidya, Matla, Hooghly, and Raimangal Rivers (photo 2.2).[5] Analysis of river-water salinity data from the monitored samples shows that water salinity in parts of the Indian Sundarbans has exceeded 25 ppt in recent years (Dasgupta et al. 2015a) (table 2.1).[6]

Flora and fauna distribution

Understanding the current distribution of flora and fauna of the Sundarbans is important as the accompanying physical, climate-related changes will have significant implications for the forest-based livelihoods of the inhabitants of the region (Chakrabarti 1987; Kumudranjau 1988; Uddin et al. 2013; United Kingdom, Department of Environment, Food and Rural Affairs 2007). Planning for appropriate adaptation will be critical for management of the Sundarbans, as well as for long-term development and poverty alleviation in adjacent areas.

The Sundarbans is known for its exceptional diversity of flora, which includes 528 species of vascular plants and many mangrove species. Although ecologically resilient, the mangrove species of the Sundarbans are highly sensitive to hydrological changes (Blasco, Saenger, and Janodet 1996), particularly to the salinity profile of the adjacent water bodies or soils. For understanding the likely impacts of water salinization on mangroves, this analytical program first developed a map of the current (2015) spatial distribution of mangrove species in the Indian Sundarbans from the Landsat 8 Operational Land Imager, Sentinel, and hyperspectral data from Hyperion corrected by field information and survey data. For the Bangladesh Sundarbans, the Bangladesh Department of Forest provided a high-resolution map of the current (2013) distribution of mangrove species (map 2.3). The vegetation map of the Bangladesh Sundarbans was produced by updating a 1997 photo-based aerial vegetation map with classified IKONOS multispectral images and detailed field data.

The Sundarbans has a rich wildlife habitat that is home to many rare and globally threatened species, including the estuarine crocodile (*Crocodilus porosus*), Royal Bengal Tiger (*Panthera tigris*), water monitor lizard (*Varanus salvator*), Gangetic dolphin (*Platinista gangetica*), and olive ridley turtle (*Lepidochelys olivacea*) (Gopal and Chauhan 2006). The region's core forest area, which is adjacent to the sea, has a low elevation. With sea-level rise, this means the imminent loss of habitat for many terrestrial and amphibian vertebrate species (IWM 2003; Loucks et al. 2010).

MAP 2.3

Mangrove species distribution in the Sundarbans

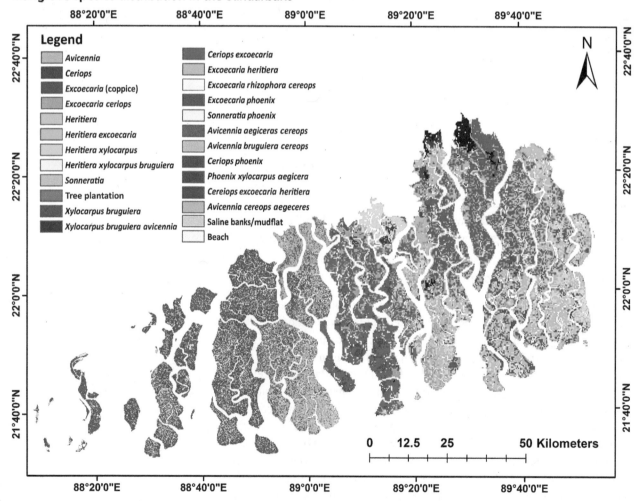

Source: Adapted from Dasgupta, Sobhan, and Wheeler 2017.

Despite wide recognition of the threat that sea-level rise poses to resident species in a changing climate, geocoded data on terrain elevation and comprehensive accounting of species are lacking, preventing a thorough vulnerability analysis for the Sundarbans. To address this gap, this analytical program drew on recent developments in species range mapping (from the Bangladesh Sundarbans, BirdLife International, and IUCN Red List threat categories) to create a geocoded high-resolution (at 0.0025 decimal degrees, or approximately 250 m), composite-species vulnerability indicator (IUCN 2015). The indicator incorporates seven subindicators based on species counts, endangered species counts, endemicity, and four measures of extinction risk. Since water salinization poses a major threat to freshwater fish, a list of fish species commonly found in the region was secured from WorldFish.

ASSESSMENT OF VULNERABILITY IN A CHANGING CLIMATE

Progressive water salinization

This study drew extensively on the World Bank's River Salinity Information System,[7] based on Dasgupta et al. (2015a). This system quantifies the prospective relationship between climate-induced changes in sea level, temperature, rainfall, and riverine flows from the Himalayas and the spread and intensity of water salinization in the coastal zone of Bangladesh, controlling for the projected land subsidence in the Ganga-Brahmaputra Delta, as well as alternative levels of upstream freshwater withdrawal. The system provided location-specific estimates of water salinity for December 2049 and 6 months (January–June) in 2050. The estimates are for 27 climate scenarios in 2050 that incorporate three global emissions scenarios (B1, A1B, A2) from the Intergovernmental Panel on Climate Change (IPCC) Fourth Assessment Report (AR4); two estimates of sea-level rise by 2050 (27 cm for scenario B1, and 32 cm for scenarios A1B and A2); three General Circulation Models (IPSL-CM4, MIROC 3.2, and ECHO-G); and three annual subsidence rates for land in the lower Ganges Delta (2, 5, and 9 mm per year).[8]

The World Bank's River Salinity Information System does not include coastal areas of West Bengal, India.[9] Therefore, to estimate future water salinity for the Indian Sundarbans, a projection model using high-resolution point data was first developed for the Bangladesh Sundarbans.[10] The findings indicate that progressive water salinization is a significant threat to the Sundarbans in a changing climate (figure 2.1). Altered riverine flows from the Himalayas due to gradual eastward meandering of the Ganges River—combined with climate-induced changes in sea level, temperature, and rainfall—will further spread and intensify river-water salinization by 2050, reaching near-ocean salinity (32 ppt) in many areas (figure 2.2). Progressive water salinization is likely to cause significant shortages of drinking water, scarcity of water for irrigation for dry-season agriculture, and significant changes in the coastal aquatic ecosystems in the Sundarbans' core forest and reclaimed areas.

FIGURE 2.1

Predicted rise in water salinization in the Bangladesh Sundarbans

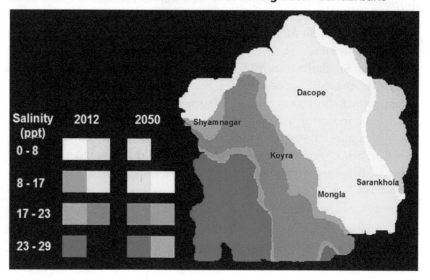

Source: Dasgupta, Sobhan, and Wheeler 2017.
Note: ppt = parts per 1,000.

FIGURE 2.2

Expected rise to near ocean-level salinity in many river sections in the Indian Sundarbans by 2050

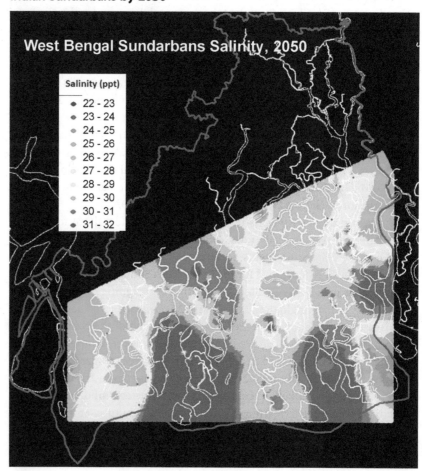

Source: Mukhopadhyay et al. 2019.
Note: ppt = parts per 1,000.

FIGURE 2.3

Projected dominance of salt-tolerant mangrove species in the Indian Sundarbans

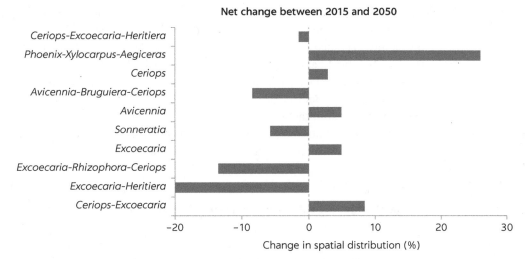

Net change between 2015 and 2050

Source: Mukhopadhyay et al. 2019.

Expected changes in flora: Dominance of salt-tolerant mangrove species

The salinity tolerance of mangrove species commonly found in the Sundarbans varies widely (Barik et al. 2018). As a result, progressive water salinization in a changing climate will lead to significant changes in the region's mangrove composition. This study used a detailed scenario analysis to assess possible impacts of climate change and sea-level rise on aquatic salinity and mangrove species.[11]

Results indicate that progressive water salinization in the Sundarbans will result in a growing dominance of salt-tolerant mangrove species at the expense of freshwater species. The salt-tolerant species and assemblages expected to dominate the landscape of the Indian Sundarbans include *Avicennia, Excoecaria, Ceriops, Avicennia-Bruguiera-Ceriops,* and *Excoecaria-Rhizophora-Ceriops.* This change will occur at the expense of freshwater species and assemblages with low-to-medium salt tolerance, including *Sonneratia, Excoecaria-Heritiera, Excoecaria-Rhizophora-Ceriops,* and *Cereops-Excoecaria-Heritiera* (figure 2.3). For the Bangladesh Sundarbans, the estimates indicate significant overall losses for *Heritiera fomes*; substantial gains for *Excoecaria agallocha*; modest changes for *Avicennia alba, A. marina, A. officinalis, Ceriops decandra,* and *Sonneratia apetala*; and mixed results for species combinations.[12]

Threats to freshwater fish species from increasing water salinization

Progressive water salinization due to sea-level rise has been identified as one of the greatest threats to freshwater fish species in the Sundarbans mangrove-forest region (see, for example, Gain, Uddin, and Sana 2008; Kasim 1979; Mandal et al. 1987; Ruby, Michael, and Mario 2010). In a changing climate, increased water salinity is expected to adversely impact their reproductive cycle and capacity; extent of suitable spawning area; and feeding, breeding, and longitudinal migration. Furthermore, no significant gain in brackish fish species is likely. Because of their feeding habits and biology, wild marine and brackish fish species prefer coastal ecosystems and thus are expected to gradually move to inland river systems over time.

This study used a detailed scenario analysis for the southwest coastal region of Bangladesh, including the Sundarbans, to assess the possible impacts of aquatic salinization on freshwater fish habitats. The analysis focused on 83 fish species found in the region that are consumed by local households. Using the salinity-tolerance range for each species and digital maps of their respective stable (12-month) habitats for 2012, 27 aquatic salinization scenarios were constructed for a changing climate in 2050. Percentage changes in habitats over the 2012–50 period indicate that brackish water will expand moderately into freshwater habitat in the western part of the region and more broadly in the eastern part (Dasgupta and Mustafa 2018). Specific fish species in the rivers at risk from progressive aquatic salinization were identified (figure 2.4).[13]

FIGURE 2.4

Range changes for subset of selected fish species in the Sundarbans by 2050

a. Salinity tolerance: 0–5 ppt

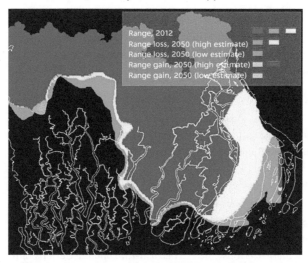

Fish Species:
Puntius sophore
Puntius ticto
Channa punctatus
Salmostoma baccila
Xenentodon cancila
Glossogobius giurus
Nemacheilus botia
Channa orientalis
Chela taubuca

b. Salinity tolerance: 5–20 ppt

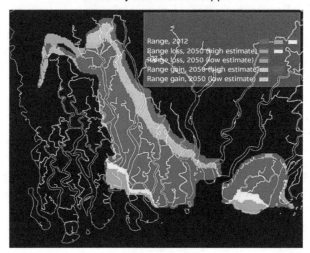

Fish Species:
Coilia ramkoranti
Cynoglossus
 cynoglossus
Harpadon nehereus
Liza parsia
Mugil cephalus
Setipinna taty
Setippina phasa
Sillago domina

Source: Dasgupta et al. 2017.
Note: High estimate: global emissions scenario A2, General Circulation Model (GCM) IPSL-CM4, sea-level rise (SLR) of 32 cm, and land subsidence of 9 mm/year; low estimate: global emissions scenario B1, GCM MIROC 3.2, SLR of 27 cm, and land subsidence of 2 mm/year (Dasgupta et al 2015a; IPCC 2007). ppt = parts per 1,000.

Threats to vertebrate species due to habitat loss from sea-level rise

As mentioned in chapter 1, the latest accounting by the IUCN (2015) reveals that 19 birds, 11 mammals, and 1 reptile in the Bangladesh Sundarbans are already regionally extinct. Since the core forest area of the Sundarbans is adjacent to the sea, with low-level ground elevation, further habitat loss for terrestrial and amphibian vertebrate species is imminent with sea-level rise. This study looked at the permanent and fragmentation impacts of inundation on the habitats of various terrestrial and amphibian vertebrate species of the Bangladesh Sundarbans, drawing on recent developments in species range mapping and alternative estimates of sea-level rise, land-subsidence, and sedimentation. It developed a high-resolution, composite-species vulnerability indicator that incorporated seven subindicators (based on species counts, endangered species counts, endemicity, and four measures of extinction risk), which it combined with alternative land-inundation scenarios to identify areas that feature both high biodiversity value and robust survival prospects as climate change continues. In the absence of definitive, location-specific subsidence and sedimentation estimates, the extent of permanent inundation of the landscape from sea-level rise is uncertain. However, it is expected that sea-level rise in a changing climate will result in significant fragmentation of habitats for many rare wildlife species (map 2.4).

MAP 2.4

Predicted fragmentation of wildlife habitat in the Bangladesh Sundarbans by 2100

a. SLR 120 cm, subsidence 35 cm, deposition 40 cm

b. SLR 120 cm, subsidence 8 cm, deposition 0 cm

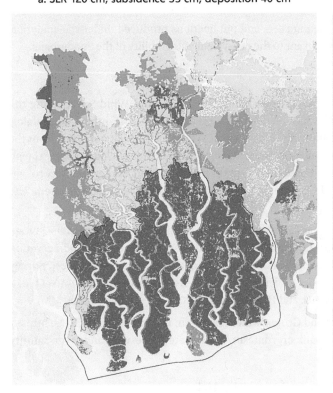 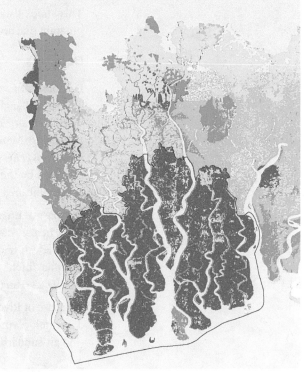

Source: Dasgupta et al. 2018.
Note: The deposition is the result of sedimentation. cm = centimeter; SLR = sea-level rise.

> "Understanding changes in water, forests, and fisheries is critical for effectively managing the Ganga Delta and the Sundarbans in a changing climate. This means that data across the entire region must be regularly collated and made freely available to scholars and practitioners, regardless of nationality. The World Bank should be congratulated for spearheading this collaborative research effort under the South Asia Water Initiative."
>
> —Sugata Hazra, professor, School of Oceanographic Studies, Jadavpur University, India

Although it would be highly desirable to protect all flora and fauna of the Sundarbans—a UNESCO World Heritage Site—resource scarcity may necessitate focusing protection on the highest-priority areas. Considering both species vulnerability and the likelihood of inundation by future sea-level rise, the highest-priority conservation status should be assigned to the Sundarbans core region, which features both high species vulnerability and the lowest likelihood of inundation in this century. This analysis also identified other critical areas in descending priority for conservation, depending on their likelihood of inundation by sea-level rise. The analysis is expected to contribute to cost-effective conservation management in the Bangladesh Sundarbans.[14]

ANNEX 2A: RELEVANT DATA SETS AND PUBLICATIONS

This annex lists the data sets and publications produced under the analytical program that are relevant to the ecosystem vulnerability of the Sundarbans.

Data sets

Database of Cyclonic Storms (Landfalls, Tracks and Wind Speed along the Tracks) in Bangladesh, West Bengal, and Odisha, 1877–2016, https://datacatalog. worldbank.org/dataset/cyclone-dataset. The database was compiled from the Bangladesh Meteorological Department, the Indian Meteorological Department, and the IBTrACS database maintained by the Global Data Center for Meteorology, operated by the US National Oceanic and Atmospheric Administration. The geographic area includes the Sundarbans.

Database of Erosion and Accretion of Bangladesh and Indian Sundarbans: 1904–2016, https://datacatalog.worldbank.org/dataset/india-erosion-and-accretion -bangladesh-and-indian-sundarbans. The database draws on mosaiced Survey of India "inch" topographical maps (1904–24), Corona space photos (1967), IRS-1D L3+Pan (2001), and IRS-R2 L4-mx (2015–16) satellite images.

Database of River and Groundwater Salinity in the Indian Sundarbans, https:// datacatalog.worldbank.org/dataset/india-water-tube-well-and-river-salinity -indian-sundarban.

Technical reports and journal articles

Cyclonic Storm Landfalls in Bangladesh, West Bengal and Odisha, 1877–2016: A Spatiotemporal Analysis, https://documents.worldbank.org/pt/publication

/documents-reports/documentdetail/904751516818659880/cyclonic-storm
-landfalls-in-bangladesh-west-bengal-and-odisha-1877-2016-a-spatiotemporal
-analysis.

Long-Term Island Area Alterations in the Indian and Bangladeshi Sundarban:
An Assessment Using Cartographic and Remote Sensing Sources, http://www
.sundarbansonline.org/wp-content/uploads/2020/03/Paper-Long-term-Island
-Area-Alterations-in-the-Indian-and-Bangladeshi-Sundarbans.pdf.

Mangrove Spatial Distribution in Indian Sundarbans: Predicting Salinity-
Induced Migration, http://www.sundarbansonline.org/wp-content/uploads
/2019/05/JMS-Mangrove-Transition-with-salinity-paper.pdf.

Sea-Level Rise and Species Conservation in Bangladesh's Sundarbans Region,
http://www.ccsenet.org/journal/index.php/jms/article/view/73348.

The Impact of Aquatic Salinization on Fish Habitats and Poor Communities in a
Changing Climate: Evidence from Southwest Coastal Bangladesh, http://www
.sundarbansonline.org/wp-content/uploads/2019/05/Ecological-Economics
-Impact-of-Climate-Change-Aquatic-Salinization-and-Fish-Habitats-and
-Poor-Community-Bangladesh-1.pdf.

The Impact of Climate Change and Aquatic Salinization on Mangrove Species
of Bangladesh Sundarbans, http://www.sundarbansonline.org/wp-content
/uploads/2019/05/SAWI-funded-Ambio-article-on-CC-and-mangroves-May
-2017.pdf.

Web feature stories

Climate Change Drives Up River Salinity in Bangladesh, https://www.thethirdpole
.net/en/2017/03/10/climate-change-drives-up-river-salinity-in-bangladesh/.

Increasing Salinity in a Changing Climate Likely to Alter Sundarbans Ecosystem,
http://www.worldbank.org/en/news/feature/2017/01/22/increasing-salinity
-in-a-changing-climate-likely-to-alter-sundarbans-ecosystem.

Will Availability of Fish Decline in Sundarbans with Climate Change? (in Bengali),
https://blogs.worldbank.org/node/25397.

NOTES

1. The estuaries of the Sundarbans are flood-dominated; that is, the duration of the northward (flood) tidal flow is less and its velocity is more than the south-directed ebb tidal current. This induces sedimentation of the interior creeks of the region and accounts for the accretion of the northern islands.
2. See the Emergency Events Database (EM-DAT), at http://www.emdat.be/database.
3. Each year, an average of 80 storms form over the world's seas; among these, about 3 occur in the North Indian Ocean Basin, comprising the Arabian Sea and the Bay of Bengal. Within the North Indian Ocean Basin, 80 percent of storm landfalls occur in the Bay of Bengal, of which about 40 percent are concentrated along its northern coasts in Bangladesh and the adjacent Indian states of Odisha and West Bengal. Despite their comparatively small number, tropical storms account for the greatest threat to the Sundarbans region. Its location near the head of the triangular shaped Bay of Bengal helps funnel seawater pushed by the wind toward the coast, causing surge amplification; the nearly sea-level elevation of the coastal lands makes the region extremely vulnerable to surge-induced inundation.
4. It is expected that the general method developed for this analysis can be applied to an extensive set of coastal locations.
5. The AZ8371 salinity tester was used to test water samples collected in the Indian Sundarbans. Samples were collected from tube wells in 50 hamlets of 27 village councils

(*gram panchayats*) and from 50 river locations. Before testing the samples collected from the field, the instrument was calibrated with distilled water, packaged drinking water, common drinking water from tube wells, and saline water after mixing salt with drinking water.

6. In the southwest coastal region of Bangladesh, soil salinity is regularly monitored at 41 stations by the Soil Research Development Institute, but soil-salinity monitoring is not common practice in the Indian Sundarbans. To fill the gap, a spatial econometric model was estimated from the results of an earlier analytical study for Bangladesh, conducted by the task team leader (Dasgupta et al. 2015b), that linked soil salinity with salinity measures for nearby rivers while controlling for land elevation, temperature, and rainfall. This study developed a method for extrapolating the Bangladesh results to estimation of geocoded soil salinity for the Indian Sundarbans, but salinity could not be estimated without high-resolution measures of land elevation. The researchers identified WorldDEM DTM, available from the Airbus Defence and Space GmbH, as being able to provide reliable elevation data for the Indian Sundarbans at €16 per 100 km². Estimation of soil salinity for the Indian Sundarbans will be feasible if funding is available for purchasing the requisite elevation data.

7. See http://sdwebx.worldbank.org/climateportal/index.cfm?page=websalinity_dynamics& ThisRegion=Asia&ThisCcode=BGD. Accessed March 2016.

8. Because the Sundarbans is located in the tidally active Ganges-Brahmaputra Delta, it is critical that simulations of future climate scenarios include projected land subsidence of the delta. Physical impacts of relative mean sea-level rise are caused by a combination of sea-level rise associated with global warming and vertical land movement (subsidence or accretion). At present, there is an intense controversy in Bangladesh regarding the estimates and projections of land subsidence in the coastal region (Dasgupta et al. 2015a). In light of the widely varying estimates, the hydrological modeling for this analysis was run for three alternative scenarios of land subsidence: 2 mm per year, 5 mm per year, and 9 mm per year.

9. The absence of location-specific data on elevation, watersheds, upstream river flows, and downstream river levels prevented hydrodynamic modeling of upstream river flows, simulation of tides, and mixing of saline tidal water with freshwater from the river systems.

10. First, the *SP* ratio (salinity in 2012 divided by salinity in 2050) was computed for each point. Next, the *SM* ratio (salinity in 2012 divided by the maximum salinity in 2012 for all points) was computed for each point. The *SP* is distributed (0, 1). Finally, fractional logit was used to estimate $SP = \beta_0 + \beta_1 SM$ for all points. This functional form preserves the (0, 1) bound, while specifying the growth rate of salinity from 2012 to 2050 at a point as a function of the gap between its current salinity and the maximum salinity in the point set (that is, effectively ocean salinity). The function fits the data extremely well. To estimate salinity in 2050 for the Indian Sundarbans, the *SM* ratio (salinity in 2012 divided by the maximum salinity in 2012 for all points) was computed for each point. Next, the regression coefficients from the Bangladesh computation above were used to estimate the *SP* ratio (salinity in 2012 divided by salinity in 2050). Finally, *SP* was used to compute salinity in 2050 and salinity in 2012 for each point.

11. To start, data on location-specific water salinity in the region were used to produce a digital map of aquatic salinity for 2012 and 27 digital maps for 2050, projected from combinations of three IPCC climate change scenarios (B1, A1B, and A2), three General Circulation Models (IPSL-CM4, MIROC 3.2, and ECHO-G), and three assumptions about the rate of subsidence in the Ganges Delta (2, 5, and 9 mm per year). Geocoded data on current water salinity were then combined with high-resolution maps of the current mangrove distribution to estimate salinity-tolerance ranges of the predominant mangrove species of the Sundarbans (for example, *Avicennia alba, A. marina, A. officinalis, Bruguiera gymnorrhiza, Ceriops decandra, Excoecaria agallocha, Heritiera fomes, Sonneratia apetala,* and *Xylocarpus mekongensis*). Finally, salinity-tolerance ranges for the mangrove species were combined with projections of location-specific water salinity for 2050 to project salinity-induced migration patterns for mangrove types—both sole species and combinations thereof.

12. The scarcity of reliable information on likely changes in location-specific elevation resulting from subsidence and sedimentation in the Sundarbans prevented this analytical program from assessing the vulnerability of mangroves to permanent inundation from climate-driven sea-level rise. Climate- or subsidence-driven sea-level rise is also an important threat factor since healthy mangroves require daily fluxes from both ocean and freshwater sources (McLeod and Salm 2006).

13. This study was conducted for the Bangladesh Sundarbans only. Analysis for the Indian Sundarbans could not be conducted, as information on fish species could not be accessed in time. The methodology developed by the study will be readily applicable to the Indian Sundarbans if data on fish species become available.

14. This study was conducted for the Bangladesh Sundarbans only. Although the study compiled data on biodiversity in the Indian Sundarbans from earlier World Bank technical assistance conducted under Sundarbans Climate Change Adaptation and Disaster Risk Management (P112693), the analysis of vulnerability of the Indian Sundarbans to sea-level rise could not be conducted because high-resolution, geocoded data on elevation of the terrain could not be accessed. Standard Digital Elevation Models available in the public domain (for example, SRTM, ASTER GDEM, and CartoDEM) record the tops of trees and houses as surface elevation and are of limited use for vulnerability analysis of the Sundarbans, where data on surface elevations stripped of vegetation and anthropogenic structures are essential. However, the investigation conducted during the study found that WorldDEM DTM, available commercially from the Airbus Defense and Space GmbH, can provide reliable elevation data.

REFERENCES

Akhter, S., M. Hasan, and Z. H. Khan. 2012. "Impact of Climate Change on Saltwater Intrusion in the Coastal Area of Bangladesh." Paper presented at the Eighth International Conference on Coastal and Port Engineering in Developing Countries, IIT Madras, Chennai, February 20–24.

Allison, M. A. 1998. "Historical Changes in the Ganges–Brahmaputra Delta Front." *Journal of Coastal Research* 14 (4): 1269–75.

Allison, M. A., and E. B. Kepple. 2001. "Modern Sediment Supply to the Lower Delta Plain of the Ganges–Brahmaputra River in Bangladesh." *Geo-Marine Letters* 21: 55–74.

Bandyopadhyay, S. 2019. *Sundarban: A Review of Evolution and Geomorphology* (in English). Washington, DC: World Bank Group.

Bandyopadhyay, S., S. Dasgupta, Z. H. Khan, and D. Wheeler. 2018a. "Cyclonic Storm Landfalls in Bangladesh, West Bengal and Odisha, 1877-2016: A Spatiotemporal Analysis." Policy Research Working Paper 8316. Washington, DC: World Bank.

Bandyopadhyay, S., N. S. Kar, S. Dasgupta, and D. Mukherjee. 2018b. "Long-Term Island Area Alternations in the India and Bangladeshi Sundarban: An Assessment Using Cartographic and Remote Sending Sources." Paper prepared for the Sundarbans Targeted Environmental Studies, South Asia Water Initiative, World Bank, Washington, DC.

Barik, J., A. Mukhopadhyay, T. Ghosh, S. K. Mukhopadhyay, S. M. Chowdhury, and S. Hazra. 2018. "Mangrove Species Distribution and Water Salinity: An Indicator Species Approach to Sundarban." *Journal of Coastal Conservation* 22 (2): 361–68.

Blasco, F., P. Saenger, and E. Janodet. 1996. "Mangroves as Indicators of Coastal Change." *Catena* 27 (3–4): 167–78.

Chakrabarti, K. 1987. "Sundarbans Honey and the Mangrove Swamps." *Journal of Bombay Natural History Society* 1: 133–37.

Chaudhuri, S., and S. Chattopadhyay. 2004. "Identification of Coasts Vulnerable for Severe Tropical Cyclones: Statistical Elucidation." *Mausam* 55 (3): 502–06.

Dasgupta, S., S. Ghosh, and D. Wheeler. 2020. "Drinking Water Salinity in Indian Sundarban" (blog). World Bank, Washington, DC. http://www.sundarbansonline.org/wp-content/uploads/2020/03/Note-Drinking-Water-Salinity-in-Indian-Sundarban.pdf.

Dasgupta, S., M. Hossain, M. Huq, and D. Wheeler. 2015b. "Climate Change and Soil Salinity: The Case of Coastal Bangladesh." *Ambio* 44 (8): 815–26.

Dasgupta, S., M. Huq, M. G. Mustafa, M. I. Sobhan, and D. Wheeler. 2017. "The Impact of Aquatic Salinization on Fish Habitats and Poor Communities in a Changing Climate: Evidence from Southwest Coastal Bangladesh." *Ecological Economics* 139 (2017): 128–39.

Dasgupta, S., M. Huq, I. Sobhan, and D. Wheeler. 2018. "Sea-Level Rise and Species Conservation in Bangladesh's Sundarbans Region." *Journal of Management and Sustainability* 8 (1).

Dasgupta, S., F. A. Kamal, Z. H. Khan, S. Choudhury, and A. Nishat. 2015a. "River Salinity and Climate Change: Evidence from Coastal Bangladesh." In *Asia and the World Economy: Actions on Climate Change by Asian Countries*, edited by John Whalley and Jiahua Pan, 205–42. Singapore: World Scientific Press.

Dasgupta, S., and G. Mustafa. 2018. "Will Availability of Fish Decline in Sundarbans with Climate Change?" (blog) (in Bengali). https://blogs.worldbank.org/node/25397.

Dasgupta, S., I. Sobhan, and D. Wheeler. 2017. "The Impact of Climate Change and Aquatic Salinization on Mangrove Species in the Bangladesh Sundarbans." *Ambio* 46 (6): 680–94.

Deo, A. A., and W. Garner. 2014. "Tropical Cyclone Activity over the Indian Ocean in the Warmer Climate." In *Monitoring and Prediction of Tropical Cyclones in the Indian Ocean and Climate Change*, edited by U. C. Mohanty, M. Mohapatra, O. P. Singh, B. K. Bandyopadhyay, and L. S. Rathore, 73–80. New York: Springer.

Field, C. D. 1995. "Impacts of Expected Climate Change on Mangroves." *Hydrobiologia* 295 (1–3): 75–81.

Gain, A. K., M. N. Uddin, and P. Sana. 2008. "Impact of River Salinity on Fish Diversity in the South-West Coastal Region of Bangladesh." *International Journal of Ecology and Environmental Sciences* 34 (1): 49–54.

Gopal, B., and M. Chauhan. 2006. "Biodiversity and Its Conservation in the Sundarban Mangrove Ecosystem." *Aquatic Sciences* 68 (3): 338–54.

IPCC (Intergovernmental Panel on Climate Change). 2007. *Climate Change 2007: The Physical Science Basis*. Contribution of Working Group I to the Fourth Assessment Report of the IPCC. New York: Cambridge University Press.

IUCN (International Union for Conservation of Nature). 2015. *Red List of Bangladesh: A Brief on Assessment Result 2015*, 24. Dhaka: IUCN.

IWM (Institute of Water Modelling). 2003. *Sundarban Biodiversity Conservation Project: Surface Water Modelling, Final Report*. Dhaka: Institute of Water Modelling, Ministry of Environment and Forests, Government of Bangladesh.

IWM (Institute of Water Modelling). 2005. "Impact Assessment of Climate Changes on the Coastal Zone of Bangladesh, Final Report." Unpublished paper. Dhaka, Institute of Water Modelling.

Kasim, H. M. 1979. "Salinity Tolerance of Certain Freshwater Fishes." Unpublished paper. Madurai Kamaraj University, Madurai, India.

Kumudranjau, N. 1988. "Economic Potentialities of the Tidal Mangrove Forests of Sundarbans in India." *Journal of the Indian Society of Coastal Research* 6 (2): 149–58.

Loucks, C., S. Barber-Meyer, M. A. Hossain, A. Barlow, and R. M. Chowdhury. 2010. "Sea Level Rise and Tigers: Predicted Impacts to Bangladesh's Sundarbans Mangroves." *Climatic Change* 98 (1): 291–98.

Mandal, S. K., M. L. Bhowmik, R. K. Chakraborty, and D. Sanfui. 1987. "A Note on Salinity Tolerance of *Liza parsia* (HAM)." *National Academy Science Letters* 10 (8).

McLeod, E., and R. V. Salm. 2006. *Managing Mangroves for Resilience to Climate Change*. Gland, Switzerland: World Conservation Union (IUCN).

Mohal, N., Z. H. Khan, and N. Rahman. 2006. *Impact of Sea level Rise on Coastal Rivers of Bangladesh*. Dhaka: Institute of Water Modelling.

Mukhopadhyay, A., D. Wheeler, S. Dasgupta, A. Dey, and I. Sobhan. 2019. "Mangrove Spatial Distribution in the Indian Sundarbans: Predicting Salinity-Induced Migration." *Journal of Management and Sustainability* 9 (1).

Nicholls, R. J., F. M. J. Hoozemans, and M. Marchand. 1999. "Increasing Flood Risk and Wetland Losses Due to Global Sea-level Rise: Regional and Global Analyses." *Global Environmental Change* 9: S69–S87.

Petersen, L., and S. Shireen. 2001. *Soil and Water Salinity in the Coastal Area of Bangladesh*. Dhaka: Bangladesh Soil Resources Development Institute.

Rahman, A. F., D. Dragoni, and B. El-Marri. 2011. "Response of the Sundarbans Coastline to Sea Level Rise and Decreased Sediment Flow: A Remote Sensing Assessment." *Remote Sensing of Environment* 115: 3121–28.

Ruby, M., M. G. Michael, and V. Mario. 2010. "*Pangasius* Juveniles Tolerate Moderate Salinity in Test." Global Aquaculture Alliance, Portsmouth, NH. http://pdf.gaalliance.org/pdf/GAA-Castaneda-March10.pdf.

Uddin, M. S., M. A. Shah, S. Khanom, and M. K. Nesha. 2013. "Climate Change Impacts on the Sundarbans Mangrove Ecosystem Services and Dependent Livelihoods in Bangladesh." *Asian Journal of Conservation Biology* 2 (2): 152–56.

United Kingdom, Department of Environment, Food, and Rural Affairs. 2007. *Investigating the Impact of Relative Sea-Level Rise on Coastal Communities and Their Livelihoods in Bangladesh*. Dhaka: Institute of Water Modelling and Center for Environment and Geographic Information Services.

3 Vulnerability of the Sundarbans Population

INTRODUCTION

As climate change continues, inundation from the increased frequency and intensity of cyclonic storms and progressive water salinization from sea-level rise are expected to have further adverse impacts on households that depend on the Sundarbans region's natural-resource base for their lives and livelihoods. This analytical activity produced one data set and seven technical reports and journal articles on assessing the vulnerability of the Sundarbans' coastal poor to climate-induced changes, with a special focus on understanding the implications of changes in water-resource productivity, availability, and quality for the most vulnerable segments of the population (women, children, and the elderly) (annex 3A).

DISPROPORTIONATE BURDEN ON THE COASTAL POOR

An analysis of population change in coastal areas of Bangladesh and Odisha and West Bengal (India) in 2000–15 indicates a significant impact of cyclones on population displacement in the two neighboring nations and a lagged adjustment process that spans several decades.[1] However, results also show that the extent of population displacement from cyclones varies greatly across coastal subregions. Displacement of coastal populations and the resulting economic disadvantages are greater in Bangladesh, compared to neighboring India, where no substantial locational effects were found (Dasgupta and Wheeler 2018).[2]

In densely populated, land-scarce countries like Bangladesh and India, poor households are disadvantaged with regard to land access, and many end up settling in low-lying regions close to the coast. The poverty map developed by the Bangladesh Bureau of Statistics, World Food Programme, and the World Bank identified 9.9 million poor people in the southwest coastal region; of these, about 60 percent (5.9 million) are extremely poor, meaning they cannot meet their basic daily nutritional requirements. Within the southwest coastal zone, many subdistricts (*upazilas*) in the Sundarbans Impact Zone[3]—Bagerhat, Barguna, Khulna, and Satkhira districts—were pinpointed as having a high incidence of poverty.

To understand the implications of climate change for the coastal poor, the task team leader of these World Bank studies conducted a GIS-based analysis in coastal Bangladesh, using poverty maps and zonal maps of storm-surge inundation and rising salinity (Dasgupta 2015) (map 3.1). In the absence of poverty maps and location-specific counts of the poor, a similar GIS analysis of poverty and climate vulnerability could not be conducted for the Indian Sundarbans. Therefore, the researchers conducted a georeferenced household survey in three geographically dispersed blocks of the Indian Sundarbans: Sagar Island, Kultali, and Gosaba.[4]

To assess the implications of intensified storm surges, the map of inundation zone from a simulated cyclone in 2050 (sea-level rise of 27 cm, increased wind speed of 10 percent, and landfall during high tide) was overlaid on the poverty map. Counts from the GIS overlays indicated that, with climate change, the total vulnerable population exposed to more than 3 m inundation depth will increase by 9 percent, but the number of poor and extremely poor people at risk will rise by 22 percent. To assess the vulnerability of Bangladesh's poor to rising salinity, the analysis focused on 2.5 million poor people in the southwest coastal region (including 1.4 million extremely poor) who are currently exposed to river-water salinity exceeding 2 ppt and are already suffering from a shortage of drinking water and scarcity of irrigation water for dry-season agriculture. Analysis of the inhabitants' exposure to the spread and increasing intensity of river-water salinization by 2050 (for alternative scenarios in a changing climate) indicates that, even in the best possible future, the total vulnerable population will increase by 15 percent, and the number of poor and extremely poor people at risk will rise by 17 percent and 23 percent, respectively (Dasgupta et al. 2015c).

Thus, the analysis concluded that poor and extremely poor people in southwest coastal Bangladesh will be disproportionately impacted by the climate change–induced threats of inundation and salinization compared to the rest of

MAP 3.1

Disproportionate exposure of Bangladesh's coastal poor to water salinity and storm surges

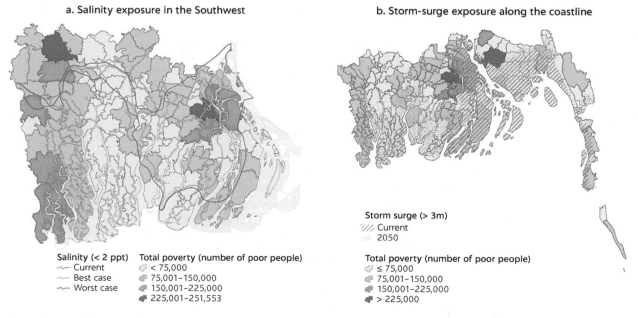

a. Salinity exposure in the Southwest

b. Storm-surge exposure along the coastline

Storm surge (> 3m)
/// Current
2050

Salinity (< 2 ppt)
~~ Current
~~ Best case
~~ Worst case

Total poverty (number of poor people)
< 75,000
75,001–150,000
150,001–225,000
225,001–251,553

Total poverty (number of poor people)
≤ 75,000
75,001–150,000
150,001–225,000
> 225,000

Source: Dasgupta 2015.
Note: m = meter; ppt = parts per 1,000.

"Multiple factors account for poverty in the Sundarbans. These World Bank–supported multidisciplinary studies, which rely on analysis of quantitative data, contribute to understanding the all-round, climate change vulnerability of poor communities in the region. This information is essential for designing programs that are responsive to the area's development challenges."

—Golam Iftekhar Mahmud, senior reporter,
Daily Prothom Alo, Bangladesh

the population. In India, findings from the georeferenced household survey suggest that poor populations in the Indian Sundarbans also have locational disadvantages. The survey results showed that high-salinity, cyclone-prone areas near the coastline have low land prices and are zones of poverty in the Sundarbans, while low-salinity areas far from the coastline with minor cyclone histories have high land prices and are zones of relative affluence. With climate change, the coastal poor will be more vulnerable to cyclone strike frequency and intensity, inundation risk, and rising salinization.

THREATS TO MOTHER-CHILD HEALTH

Increased salinity in drinking water

Progressive salinization of rivers and groundwater has resulted in the decline of available fresh drinking water (box 3.1). This situation will likely have numerous adverse effects on mother-child health, including dehydration, hypertension, prenatal complications, and increased infant mortality. A survey of the literature has identified several micro-level studies conducted in the coastal region of Bangladesh that have assessed the impact of drinking water salinity on hypertension in pregnant women (Khan et al. 2008, 2011; Naser et al. 2019; Scheelbeek et al. 2016; Vineis, Chan, and Khan 2011). These studies draw on numerous international observational studies and clinical trials that established a strong link between higher salt intake and elevated blood pressure (Alderman 2000; Calabrese and Tuthill 1981; Hallenbeck, Brenniman, and Anderson 1981; He and MacGregor 2007; Midgley et al. 1996; Welty et al. 1986). More recently, Dasgupta, Huq, and Wheeler (2016) and Joseph et al. (2019) performed econometric panel studies using Bangladesh Demographic and Health Surveys to estimate the effect of drinking water salinity on infant mortality. Controlling for many other determinants of infant mortality, Dasgupta, Huq, and Wheeler (2016) found high significance for mothers' salinity exposure during the last month of pregnancy and no significance for exposure during the preceding months on mortality probability for infants under 2 months old. The implied impact on infant mortality is comparable in magnitude to the estimated effects of traditionally cited variables (for example, maternal age and education, gender of household head, household wealth, toilet facilities, drinking water sources, and cooking fuels). Using nonparametric regression, Joseph et al. (2019) reported higher infant mortality (death within 2 months, as well as 12 months, after birth) when drinking water salinity is high.

BOX 3.1

Drinking water shortage from salinization of rivers and groundwater

In the Indian Sundarbans, drinking water comes mostly from deep tube wells. Water is not potable if its salinity exceeds 1 part per 1,000 (ppt), but recent field measurements conducted by this analytical program study found that salinity in deep tube-well water exceeds 1 ppt in 17 of 50 hamlets in Gosaba, Hingalgunj, and Patharpratima blocks of the Sundarbans Reclaimed Region in India. The highest salinity, at 4.68 ppt, was recorded in Karikarpara Hamlet of Hingalgunj Block (map B3.1.1a).

In populated areas of the Indian Sundarbans, groundwater from deep aquifers is the main source of drinking water. In the western portion, only the Hugli and Baratala (or Muriganga) rivers, linked to the Hugli's west-bank tributaries and the Ganga River, still bring freshwater to Sagar and Namkhana blocks. Five other major rivers flowing through the central and eastern parts of the region—the Saptamukhi, Thakuran, Matla, Bidya, and Raimangal—have lost their upstream connections with the Ganga, their freshwater source, and are tidally fed. A baseline profile of river-water salinity, put together from field measurements taken by the Nature Environment and Wildlife Society

(NEWS) and World Wildlife Fund–India (WWF-India), has also found many areas with elevated river-water salinity—as high as 25 ppt in some cases (map B3.1.1b).[a] Water from shallow aquifers nearby is undrinkable due to high salinity. Currently, drinking water comes solely from deep tube wells that lift water from aquifers at a 900-foot depth or more. With climate change, these are becoming increasingly saline as upstream freshwater diminishes and ocean water diffuses further inland.

In the Bangladesh Sundarbans, monitored data on groundwater salinity are sparse. However, the World Bank's River Salinity Information System projects that progressive water salinization in the Sundarbans ecosystem will lead to a significant decline in the availability of drinking water from river sources in the Sundarbans Impact Zone. Even in the best-case 2050 scenario, freshwater (0–1 ppt) zones in these rivers will be lost entirely in Khulna and Barguna districts in the dry season. In Pirojpur and Bagerhat districts, they will decline by 81 percent and 71 percent, respectively, and, in the worst-case scenario, by 100 percent and 93 percent.

MAP B3.1.1

Water salinity in the Indian Sundarbans, February and May 2019

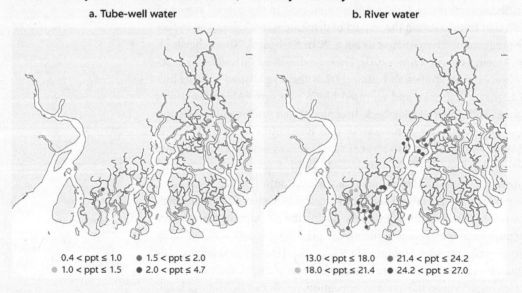

a. Tube-well water

b. River water

Source: Adapted from Dasgupta, Ghosh, and Wheeler 2020a.
Note: ppt = parts per 1,000.

continued

Box 3.1, *continued*

In the early years of Sundarbans settlement, villagers kept ponds for common use, and rainwater collected in those ponds provided year-round drinking water. With the introduction of tube wells, the village ponds were gradually put to other uses. Unfortunately, many can no longer be restored because the supporting institutional mechanisms for their upkeep have been lost. The reality is that packaged drinking water in remote locations is unaffordable for most local people.

Source: Dasgupta, Ghosh, and Wheeler 2020a.
Note: ppt = parts per 1,000.
a. Field measurements taken by this study team found river-water salinity in a range of 13–27 ppt near villages.

Malnutrition from reduction in wild freshwater fish

South Asia still has the world's largest prevalence of anemia, particularly among women of reproductive age. Also, more than half of the region's children are underweight (a substandard weight-to-height ratio) or stunted (a substandard height-to-age ratio). In India alone, the prevalence of anemia is 51.5 percent (2016 figure), mostly among pregnant women (Kalaivani and Premachandran 2018); for children under the age of five, 21 percent are underweight and 38 percent are stunted (2016 figures) (Development Initiatives 2018). In Bangladesh, 39.6 percent of women of reproductive age suffer from anemia (2016 figure); for children under five, 14.4 percent are underweight and 36.2 percent are stunted (2014 figures).[5,6] The problem is even more serious in the Sundarbans, where millions of people are poor and cannot meet basic daily nutritional requirements. Chronic and acute malnutrition among children in coastal Bangladesh, as indicated by statistics on underweight and stunted children, are higher than the thresholds set by the World Health Organization (WHO) for public-health emergencies (Bangladesh, Ministry of Health and Family Welfare 2011).

In this context, including fish in the household diet is critical for poor households (Dasgupta et al. 2017b). In coastal Bangladesh and India, fish are naturally abundant throughout the year and are more affordable than other animal-source foods (photo 3.1). Importantly, fish are the largest source of high-quality protein and are a major source of minerals and micronutrients that are difficult to obtain in sufficient amounts from plant-based foods (Kent 1987; Michaelsen et al. 2011; Murphy and Allen 2003; Roos, Islam, and Thilsted 2003). Nutritional research has documented numerous health benefits from fish-intensive diets, including higher concentrations of bioavailable minerals and vitamins, essential fatty acids, animal protein, and micronutrients (Bogard 2017; Bogard et al. 2015; Kawarazuka and Bene 2011; Wheal et al. 2016). Vitamin B12, found only in animal-food sources, lowers preterm delivery and supports physical development, various brain functions, and nervous system maintenance (FAO and WHO 2004).[7]

This study analyzed the progressive salinization of rivers in coastal Bangladesh in a changing climate, using poverty maps overlaid with maps of fish-species gains and losses. The results show adverse impacts for freshwater fish habitats in the southwest coastal region, including the Sundarbans Impact Zone. A comparative analysis of habitats for 83 fish species commonly found in local diets over the 2012–50 period indicates that, in areas with poor populations, the prevalence of species loss is six times greater than species gain (figure 3.1).[8]

PHOTO 3.1

Significance of fish in the household diet

Source: © Pritthijit (Raja) Kundu. Reproduced with permission from Pritthijit (Raja) Kundu; further permission required for reuse.

FIGURE 3.1

Predicted losses of freshwater fish habitats in poor areas, 2012–50

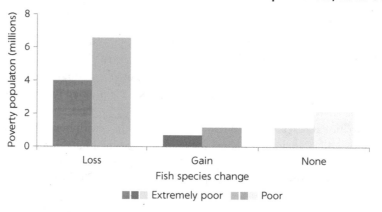

Source: Adapted from Dasgupta et al. 2017a.

Among the subdistricts exhibiting the top 10 species-loss indicators, three are found in the Sundarbans Impact Zone: Bagerhat, Morrelganj, and Rampal (Dasgupta and Mustafa 2018). For millions of poor and extremely poor people in the region, wild freshwater fish are the main source of dietary protein and essential micronutrients, making this finding serious.[9] The stakes are particularly high for children (Wheeler et al. 2017) and pregnant women since protein, mineral, and micronutrient deficiencies can lead to increased mortality risk and reduced immunity to disease.

Determining regional variations: Timing and magnitude of water-cycle impacts

This analytical program also sought to gain a better understanding of regional variations in mother-child health in order to suggest more effective policy measures for narrowing gaps in health outcomes. Using more than 100,000 records of the India National Family Health Survey (NFHS-4) for 2015–16 and the Bangladesh Demographic and Health Survey for 2011, the study team conducted econometric research that explored determinants of regional variations in maternal anemia and underweight children for Bangladesh and the neighboring Indian states of West Bengal, Bihar, and Jharkhand.

Results show that, even after explaining variations in the probability of maternal anemia and child wasting due to commonly cited determinants (for example, mother's age, mother's education, household wealth, and child birth order), significant interregional variations remain (map 3.2). These variations are explained by spatial clustering of health services, political instability, religious culture, and flood-proneness—a proxy for the relative prices of fish and milk, as well as the relative scarcity of clean water for drinking, food preparation, and washing (Dasgupta and Wheeler 2019a).

By highlighting the importance of local differences in the timing and magnitude of water-cycle impacts for regional variations in mother-child health outcomes, this activity drew attention to the critical role of environmental conditions—previously ignored in the literature and policy dialogue on malnutrition. Remarkably, the research suggests that regional and temporal variations in the water cycle through flood and drought conditions affect mother-child health as strongly as more commonly cited socioeconomic factors.[10]

MAP 3.2

Regional differences in mother-child health unexplained by commonly cited determinants

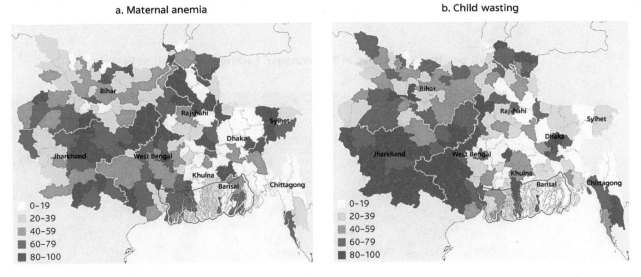

Source: Dasgupta and Wheeler 2019b.
Note: The number ranges shown in the legends, scaled from 0 to 100, indicate standardized mean residuals for districts resulting from the regression analysis using commonly cited determinants.

The current scientific consensus holds that, in a changing climate, changes in temperature-related evapotranspiration rates, altered meltwater flows from mountain regions, and increasingly erratic monsoons (with more severe drought conditions in some subregions and greater flooding in others) will magnify regional and temporal variations in the water cycle of the Ganga-Brahmaputra Basin, calling for improved flood and drought management. Sensitivity to flood-proneness makes mother-child health vulnerable to varying patterns of extreme weather events with climate change. Better outcomes may depend on more effective planning for water-resource allocation. Cooperative basinwide planning would involve closer coordination between India and Bangladesh, as well as the basin subregions within each country.

THREATS TO HEALTH AND LIVELIHOODS FROM SALINITY-INDUCED IMPACTS

Prawn postlarvae catching

For poorly educated women in the Sundarbans, prawn postlarvae (PPL) catching for aquaculture firms is an important occupational choice, requiring the catcher to wade waist-deep in salty water for hours, dragging triangular nets (photo 3.2).[11] Also, the rivers and creeks where the catchers work are infested with crocodiles (*Crocodylus palustris*), and activities are fraught with risk of attack by tigers, venomous snakes, and sharks. For their catch, the women are paid only low piece rates. Alongside the risks of wildlife attack and poverty, anecdotal accounts suggest that long-term saline immersion poses serious health risks, an issue that has received little research attention.

This analytical program conducted focus group interviews with local leaders of Women's Self-Help Groups in 15 gram-panchayats of the Indian Sundarbans. Based on focus group discussions, a survey of 900 households was conducted to collect information on the livelihood activities of women who spend long hours wading in saline water, their average saline exposure time, and illnesses. Afterward, local doctors in all gram panchayats were consulted to verify the

PHOTO 3.2

Prawn postlarvae catching in Shyamnagar, Satkhira, and sorting in Hingalganj, North 24 Parganas

Sources: © Md. Istiak Sobhan / World Bank (left); © Santadas Ghosh (right). Reproduced with permission; further permission required for reuse.

incidence of illnesses. The information was later analyzed to investigate the relationships between salinity, saline-immersive fishing activity, and self-reported and measured health problems.

The study findings highlight the economics of occupational choice. The opportunity wage, proxied by years of education, together with child-rearing obligations, proxied by a household's ratio of children to working-age women, are sufficient variables for distinguishing between women who have no engagement in PPL catching and those with many years of engagement. For women with a secondary education and high child-care demands, engagement in PPL catching is virtually zero. Conversely, engagement is substantial for women with no formal education (that is, with low opportunity wages) and no child-care demands.

To investigate the health consequences, the study team drew on self-reported health problems from a list of 67 ailments identified by the surveyed women. Those women who engage in saline-immersive PPL catching reported significantly more health problems than their counterparts who engage in otherwise comparable low-wage economic activities. Statistical analysis later revealed that their health problems are clustered in a subset of the 67 ailments enumerated by the survey: irregular menstruation, eyesight problems, gastric pain, pain in hands and legs, knee pain, skin allergies, and itching.

In sum, this study revealed a poverty-environment nexus that affects the health and livelihoods of more than 100,000 women in the Indian Sundarbans.[12] The areas where PPL catching is still prevalent are remote from market centers and offer few alternative occupations for less-educated women. In contrast, women elsewhere in the Sundarbans, who have access to better transport facilities and markets, have started home-based work alternatives (for example, food processing, tailoring, and embroidery). Therefore, it is expected that more women in isolated areas will leave PPL catching for these work alternatives if appropriate policies promote new business lines, facilitate skills training, and provide subsidized credit. The benefits for these women will be significantly improved health and better livelihoods (Dasgupta, Ghosh, and Wheeler 2020b).

Dry-season rice irrigation

Agriculture is an important sector in Bangladesh, contributing up to 13 percent of gross domestic product and employing 41 percent of the labor force (2016–17 figures). In 2018–19, the country produced 36.4 million tons of rice, including 19.6 million tons of winter (*Boro*) rice. Production of winter rice is conditional on the availability of an adequate water supply for irrigation with salinity of less than 2 ppt. In a worst-case future scenario for the Sundarbans Impact Zone, river water will no longer be utilizable for Boro-rice irrigation in Barguna and Khulna districts. Even in the best-case future scenario, scarcity of water for irrigation will be severe. For example, in Khulna District, 98 percent of the rivers will be adversely affected. In addition, rising soil salinity will adversely impact Boro yields, with expected adverse impacts on the livelihoods of the region's Boro farmers.[13] River water in the Indian Sundarbans is too saline for rice irrigation. Groundwater, generally used for Boro rice irrigation, has also started to show increasing salinity (photo 3.3).

PHOTO 3.3
Rice winnowing in Gosaba, South 24 Parganas

Source: © Pritthijit (Raja) Kundu. Reproduced with permission from Pritthijig (Raja) Kundu; further permission required for reuse.

Effects of altered mangrove composition and forest decline

In the Bangladesh Sundarbans, salinity-induced changes in the composition of mangroves will have a strong regressive impact on livelihood options for the poor (Dasgupta, Sobhan, and Wheeler 2017). For example, in Shyamnagar, the region's poorest upazila (subdistrict), where current salinity precludes *Heritiera fomes* (a high-value timber species), large losses are expected for *Avicennia alba, A. marina, A. officinalis, Ceriops decandra*, and *Sonneratia apetala*. In Koyra, another poor upazila by national standards and the second-poorest in the Sundarbans mangrove region, it is expected that a large loss in *H. fomes* will be partially offset by gains in *A. alba, A. marina, A. officinalis, C. decandra*, and *S. apetala*. Although expected growth of *A. officinalis, C. decandra*, and *S. apetala* in the forest areas will augment potential for honey production, it may further increase human-wildlife conflicts, as deaths of honey collectors from tiger attacks are already quite common.

For the Indian Sundarbans, poverty maps and counts are unavailable; however, discussion with local experts indicates that salinity-induced changes in the composition of mangrove species are already affecting livelihoods.[14] For honey collectors, livelihood options are adversely impacted by a decline in the growth of forest land and mangrove species, along with reduced productivity of forest sites. Currently, the first honey of the season, collected from *Aegiceras* and *Acanthus* sp., fetches a high value, at Rs. 200–250 per kilogram (kg). Honey collected later in the season, mainly from *Ceriops* and *Avicennia* sp., fetches less (Rs. 80–120 per kg). With changes in mangrove-species combinations, the fragrance and viscosity of honey—and thus its price—will vary.[15]

Reduction in freshwater fisheries

Fisheries constitute an important livelihood source for tens of thousands of poor people in the coastal region of Bangladesh and India living near the Sundarbans

PHOTO 3.4

Fishing in Gosaba and Patharpratima, South 24 Parganas

Source: © Ajanta Dey. Reproduced with permission from Ajanta Dey; further permission required for reuse.

mangrove forest (photo 3.4). In the Indian Sundarbans, the current salinity of rivers and creeks exceeds the tolerance threshold of most freshwater fish species. Rivers in the eastern Bangladesh Sundarbans are comparatively less saline. However, it is feared that, with sea-level rise and progressive water salinization in a changing climate, the reduced availability of freshwater fish species will adversely affect the livelihoods of households dependent on freshwater fishing in the Bangladesh Sundarbans (Chowdhury, Sukhan, and Hannan 2010; Gain, Uddin, and Sana 2008). In the Sundarbans Impact Zone, increased water salinity will impact habitats for freshwater fish (Dasgupta 2017), substantially reducing freshwater (capture) fisheries. For the districts of Khulna, Bagerhat, and Satkhira, in a best-case future scenario, the expected declines in optimum river area for *Catla catla, Labeo rohita,* and *Cirrhinus cirrhosis* are 49 percent, 20 percent, and 15 percent, respectively; for optimum wild habitat for *Macrobrachium rosenbergii,* the expected declines are 88 percent, 35 percent, and 14 percent. For these three districts, in a worst-case future scenario, the respective declines in optimum habitat for *C. catla, L. rohita,* and *C. cirrhosis* are 100 percent, 81 percent, and 34 percent; for *M. rosenbergii,* they are 97 percent, 57 percent, and 26 percent.[16] Significant changes in small freshwater species in the wild (for example, *Eutropiichthys vacha, Cirrhinus reba, Chela laubuca, Mystus vittatus, Ailia coila, Cynoglossus lingua,* and *Salmostoma bacalia*) are also probable (Dasgupta and Mustafa 2018).

OUT-MIGRATION OF WORKING-AGE ADULTS

For the Bangladesh Sundarbans, results of this analytic program and earlier studies using demographic-survey data show that households threatened by inundation and salinization—particularly those unprotected by polders (embankments) and relatively isolated from market centers—respond by "hollowing out." Economic necessity drives more working-age adults, particularly males, to seek outside earnings. At the same time, out-migration–induced impacts increase the incidence of poverty for the population left behind, at least for a significant period (Dasgupta et al. 2015b) (photo 3.5). Given that the affected population has very low levels of human capital, the time needed for migrant family members to save sufficient funds to send remittances home may be considerable.[17, 18]

PHOTO 3.5

Staggering poverty in the Sundarbans

Source: © Anamitra Anurag Danda. Reproduced with permission from Anamitra Anurag Danda; further permission required for reuse.

This study's powerful results for polder protection and market access suggest that investment in both transport and transportation infrastructure that incorporates key ecological concerns is an attractive option for low-lying coastal areas. At present, inhabitants of isolated settlements travel up to 14 hours to reach market centers. According to this study's econometric findings for poverty incidence, transport-network improvements would allow people to more easily ship their products to market, contributing to poverty alleviation and enhanced resilience.

In the Indian Sundarbans, a comparable analysis of livelihood threats and out-migration could not be conducted due to the unavailability of location-specific data on poverty, elevation, and salinity in the Sundarbans Reclaimed Region. In the absence of such data, the study team conducted a survey in Sagar, Kultali, and Gosaba blocks of West Bengal, combined with environmental data, to examine the relationships between land prices, household incomes, and climate change–related factors. The findings show that high-salinity, cyclone-prone areas near the coastline are poverty zones, while low-salinity areas far from the coastline with minor cyclone histories are zones of relative affluence (Bandyopadhyay et al. 2019).

In a simulation exercise, the study found that switching the risk of salinity, cyclonic-storm intensity, and inundation from the most to the least favorable setting caused a sharp drop in land prices and household income, each falling from the 90th to the 10th percentile. Therefore, it can be expected that the combined risk of cyclone strike frequency and intensity, progressive salinization, and inundation in a changing climate will impact the poorest, most vulnerable residents of the Indian Sundarbans, who will be the last ones to flee as the sea moves steadily inland.

"For millions of people that live in the Sundarbans, development opportunities are limited. Livelihoods suffer from frequent natural disasters, such as Cyclone Amphan, which recently devastated the region. Climate change assessments project an increase in such disasters. The multidisciplinary studies conducted by the World Bank on issues for which available evidence is limited provide a solid foundation for discussion of targeted interventions for vulnerability reduction in the Sundarbans."

—J. M. Mauskar, advisor, Observer Research Foundation
and former special secretary, Ministry of Environment,
Forest and Climate Change, India

ANNEX 3A: RELEVANT DATA SET AND PUBLICATIONS

This annex lists the data set and publications produced under the analytical program that are relevant to vulnerability of the Sundarbans population.

Data set

Database of River and Groundwater Salinity in the Indian Sundarbans, https://datacatalog.worldbank.org/dataset/india-water-tube-well-and-river-salinity-indian-sundarban.

Technical reports and journal articles

Climate Change, Livelihood Threats, and Household Responses in Bangladesh Sundarbans, http://www.sundarbansonline.org/wp-content/uploads/2019/05/SAWI-funded-Climate-Change-Livelihood-Threats-and-Household-Responses-in-the-Bangladesh-Sundarbans-1.pdf.

Discounting Disaster: Land Markets and Climate Change in the Indian Sundarbans, http://www.sundarbansonline.org/wp-content/uploads/2020/03/Paper-Land-Markets-and-Climate-Change-in-the-Indian-Sundarbans.pdf.

Explaining Regional Variations in Mother-Child Health: Environmental Determinants in India and Bangladesh, http://www.sundarbansonline.org/wp-content/uploads/2020/03/Paper-Explaining-Regional-Variations-in-Mother-Child-Health-Role-of-Environmental-Factors-.pdf based on Accounting for Regional Differences in Mother and Child Health: Bangladesh, West Bengal, Bihar and Jharkhand, http://documents.worldbank.org/curated/en/825161553796198653/Accounting-for-Regional-Differences-in-Mother-and-Child-Health-Bangladesh-West-Bengal-Bihar-and-Jharkhand.

Fishing in Saltier Waters: Climate Change, Saline Exposure and Women's Health in the Indian Sundarbans (unpublished paper).

Mangrove Spatial Distribution in Indian Sundarbans: Predicting Salinity-Induced Migration, http://www.sundarbansonline.org/wp-content/uploads/2019/05/JMS-Mangrove-Transition-with-salinity-paper.pdf.

The Cyclone's Shadow: Historical Storm Impacts and Population Displacement in Bangladesh, West Bengal, and Odisha, https://www.sundarbansonline.org/wp-content/uploads/2019/05/Paper-Historical-Storm-Impacts-and-Population-Displacement-1.pdf.

The Impact of Aquatic Salinization on Fish Habitats and Poor Communities in a Changing Climate: Evidence from Southwest Coastal Bangladesh, http://www .sundarbansonline.org/wp-content/uploads/2019/05/Ecological-Economics -Impact-of-Climate-Change-Aquatic-Salinization-and-Fish-Habitats-and -Poor-Community-Bangladesh-1.pdf.

The Impact of Climate Change and Aquatic Salinization on Mangrove Species of Bangladesh Sundarbans, http://www.sundarbansonline.org/wp-content /uploads/2019/05/SAWI-funded-Ambio-article-on-CC-and-mangroves-May -2017.pdf.

The Socioeconomics of Fish Consumption and Child Health: An Observational Cohort Study in Bangladesh, https://elibrary.worldbank.org/doi/abs/10.1596 /1813-9450-8217.

Web feature stories

Drinking Water in the Indian Sundarbans, https://www.sundarbansonline.org /wp-content/uploads/2020/03/Note-Drinking-Water-Salinity-in-Indian -Sundarban.pdf.

May Our Children Always Have Fish and Rice! (in Bengali), https://blogs .worldbank.org/node/25438.

The Perils of Prawn-Catching for Women in Sundarbans, https://www .sundarbansonline.org/wp-content/uploads/2020/03/Note-Perils-of-Prawn -PL-Catching-in-Sundarban.pdf.

Increasing Salinity in a Changing Climate Likely to Alter Sundarbans Ecosystem, http://www.worldbank.org/en/news/feature/2017/01/22/increasing-salinity -in-a-changing-climate-likely-to-alter-sundarbans-ecosystem.

Will Availability of Fish Decline in Sundarbans with Climate Change? (in Bengali), https://blogs.worldbank.org/node/25397.

NOTES

1. This process refers to adjustments made by households to contemporaneous and past cyclone impacts, as well as locational economic factors and government policies that compensated households for cyclone damage and disadvantages related to location.
2. It is possible that India's extensive compensation programs in Odisha and West Bengal may have significantly dampened the responsiveness of population dynamics to both cyclones and locational disadvantages.
3. The Sundarbans Impact Zone of Bangladesh consists of areas within 20 km of the Sundarbans Reserve Forest perimeter, and are in Barguna, Bagerhat, Khulna, Pirojpur, and Satkhira districts.
4. These three blocks were selected for their differences in change dynamics. Sagar and Gosaba comprise islands only and are inaccessible by land transportation. Sagar is an important destination for religious and beach tourism. Gosaba has experienced some growth in ecotourism, which provides livelihood opportunities beyond direct dependence on the land or fishing. In Kultali, increased settlement has been accompanied by a reduction in agricultural land and orchards, while dense forests have increased marginally. Gosaba, by contrast, has experienced a reduction in dense forests and aquaculture and an expansion in settlements, agricultural land, and orchards. Sagar has seen extensive land erosion; settlements, aquaculture, and forest densification have increased, while agricultural lands have receded.
5. Index Mundi, Bangladesh: Prevalence of Anemia. For more information, see https://www .indexmundi.com/facts/bangladesh/prevalence-of-anemia.

6. UNICEF (United Nations International Children's Fund) Data, Monitoring the Situation of Children and Women. For more information, see https://data.unicef.org/topic/nutrition /malnutrition.

7. A recent analysis of more than 36,000 records from successive Bangladesh Demographic and Health Surveys indicates that mothers' dietary preferences for fish and the seasonal availability of fish during prepartum and postpartum periods significantly affect child mortality and resistance to several common childhood illnesses.

8. This study was conducted for the Bangladesh Sundarbans only. Analysis for the Indian Sundarbans could not be conducted as information on fish could not be accessed on time.

9. In Bangladesh, the importance of fishery resources for the food security of the poor is widely acknowledged, and the fisheries and aquaculture sector features prominently in the national development agenda (Bangladesh, Ministry of Food and Disaster Management 2006, 2011). Using nationally representative data on changes in fish consumption in 2000–10, Toufique and Belton (2014) highlight the pro-poor impact of aquaculture growth, which has lowered fish prices and increased fish consumption. Between 1991 and 2010, total fish consumption increased by 30 percent. However, aquaculture, which is designed to maximize productivity, has not led to a proportionate gain in dietary diversity, micronutrient intake, and food and nutrition security, particularly for poor consumers (Belton, Asseldonk, and Thilsted 2014). Bogard et al. (2017) report significant declines in iron and calcium intake from fish, and no significant change in intake of zinc, vitamin A, and vitamin B12. Until aquaculture achieves parity with capture fishery in promoting dietary diversity and micronutrient intake, enhancing capture-fisheries access for the poor will remain important for their food and nutrition security.

10. In a comparison of predicted probabilities for maternal anemia and child wasting, this study finds that the poorest, least-educated mothers and their children in a district with the most favorable values for health services, instability, and flood-proneness have better health outcomes than their wealthiest, best-educated counterparts in a district with the least favorable values.

11. Wild tiger-prawn seedlings.

12. PPL catching is also an important occupation for women living near the Bangladesh Sundarbans.

13. Earlier research estimated an output decline of 15.6 percent for HYV-Boro in nine subdistricts where soil salinity will exceed 4 decisiemens (dS) per m before 2050 (Dasgupta et al. 2015a).

14. Increasing salinity will also reduce the diversity of mangrove species, which could diminish the attraction of the Sundarbans as a biodiversity hotspot destination.

15. Altered mangrove composition may also reduce the availability of fuelwood for household use and thus increase women's fuelwood-collection time.

16. For Barguna District in a worst-case scenario, the expected decline in optimum wild habitat for *M. rosenbergii* is 14 percent.

17. The results of this empirical study show that the critical zone for climate risk lies within 4 km of the coast and tidal rivers, with attenuated impacts for coastal zone households located at higher elevations and protected by polders.

18. For a similar analysis of the southwest coastal region of Bangladesh, see Dasgupta et al. (2016).

REFERENCES

Alderman, M. H. 2000. "Salt, Blood Pressure, and Human Health." *Hypertension* 36: 890–93.

Bandyopadhyay, S., S. Bandyopadhyay, S. Dasgupta, C. Mallik, and D. Wheeler. 2019. "Discounting Disaster: Land Markets and Climate Change in the Indian Sundarbans." Paper prepared for the Sundarbans Targeted Environmental Studies, South Asia Water Initiative, World Bank, Washington, DC.

Bangladesh, Ministry of Food and Disaster Management. 2006. *National Food Policy*. Dhaka: Ministry of Food and Disaster Management.

Bangladesh, Ministry of Food and Disaster Management. 2011. *Country Investment Plan: A Roadmap towards Investment in Agriculture, Food Security and Nutrition*. Dhaka: Ministry of Food and Disaster Management.

Bangladesh, Ministry of Health and Family Welfare. 2011. *HPNSDP: Strategic Plan for Health Population and Nutrition Sector Development Program 2011–2016*. Dhaka: Government of Bangladesh. http://www.bma.org.bd/pdf/strategic_Plan_HPNSDP_2011-16.pdf.

Belton, B., I. J. M. Van Asseldonk, and S. H. Thilsted. 2014. "Faltering Fisheries and Ascendant Aquaculture Implications for Food and Nutrition Security in Bangladesh." *Food Policy* 44: 77–87.

Bogard, J. R. 2017. "The Contribution of Fish to Nutrition and Food Security: Informing the Evidence Base for Agricultural Policy in Bangladesh." PhD thesis, Faculty of Medicine, University of Queensland, Australia.

Bogard, J. R., G. C. Marks, A. Mamun, and S. H. Thilsted. 2017. "Non-farmed Fish Contribute to Greater Micronutrient Intakes Than Farmed Fish: Results from an Intra-household Survey in Rural Bangladesh." *Public Health Nutrition* 20 (4): 702–11.

Bogard, J. R., S. H. Thilsted, G. C. Marks, M. A. Wahab, M. A. R. Hossain, J. Jakobsen, and J. Stangoulis. 2015. "Nutrient Composition of Important Fish Species in Bangladesh and Potential Contribution to Recommended Nutrient Intakes." *Journal of Food Composition and Analysis* 42: 120–33.

Calabrese, E. J., and R. W. Tuthill. 1981. "The Influence of Elevated Levels of Sodium in Drinking Water on Elementary and High School Students in Massachusetts." *Science of the Total Environment* 18: 117–33.

Chowdhury, M. T., Z. P. Sukhan, and M. A. Hannan. 2010. "Climate Change and Its Impact on Fisheries Resource in Bangladesh." *Proceedings of International Conference on Environmental Aspects of Bangladesh*, Japan, September.

Dasgupta, S. 2015. "Left Unattended 5.3 Million of Bangladesh's Poor Will Be Vulnerable to the Effects of Climate Change in 2050." *Let's Talk Development* (blog), April 6. World Bank, Washington, DC. blogs.worldbank.org/developmenttalk/left-unattended-53-million -bangladesh-s-poor-will-be-vulnerable-effects-climate-change-2050.

Dasgupta, S. 2017. "Increasing Salinity in a Changing Climate Likely to Alter Sundarban's Ecosystem" (feature story). January 22. https://www.worldbank.org/en/news/feature /2017/01/22/increasing-salinity-in-a-changing-climate-likely-to-alter-sundarbans -ecosystem.

Dasgupta, S., S. Ghosh, and D. Wheeler. 2020a. "Drinking Water Salinity in Indian Sundarban" (blog). World Bank, Washington, DC. http://www.sundarbansonline.org/wp-content /uploads/2020/03/Note-Drinking-Water-Salinity-in-Indian-Sundarban.pdf.

Dasgupta, S., S. Ghosh, and D. Wheeler. 2020b. "Perils of Prawn-Catching for Women in Sundarbans." World Bank, Washington, DC. http://www.sundarbansonline.org/wp-content /uploads/2020/03/Note-Perils-of-Prawn-PL-Catching-in-Sundarban.pdf.

Dasgupta, S., M. Hossain, M. Huq, and D. Wheeler. 2015a. "Climate Change and Soil Salinity: The Case of Coastal Bangladesh." *Ambio* 44 (8): 815–26.

Dasgupta, S., M. Hossain, M. Huq, and D. Wheeler. 2015b. "Climate Change, Livelihood Threats, and Household Response in the Bangladesh Sundarbans." Paper prepared for the Sundarbans Targeted Environmental Studies, South Asia Water Initiative, World Bank, Washington, DC.

Dasgupta, S., M. Hossain, M. Huq, and D. Wheeler. 2016. "Facing the Hungry Tide: Climate Change, Livelihood Threats and Household Responses in Coastal Bangladesh." *Climate Change Economics* 7 (3): 1–25.

Dasgupta, S., M. Huq, M. G. Mustafa, M. I. Sobhan, and D. Wheeler. 2017a. "The Impact of Aquatic Salinization on Fish Habitats and Poor Communities in a Changing Climate: Evidence from Southwest Coastal Bangladesh." *Ecological Economics* 139 (2017): 128–39.

Dasgupta, S., M. Huq, and D. Wheeler. 2016. "Drinking Water Salinity and Infant Mortality in Coastal Bangladesh." *Water Economics and Policy* 2 (1).

Dasgupta, S., F. A. Kamal, Z. H. Khan, S. Choudhury, and A. Nishat. 2015c. "River Salinity and Climate Change: Evidence from Coastal Bangladesh." In *Asia and the World Economy: Actions on Climate Change by Asian Countries*, edited by John Whalley and Jiahua Pan, 205 –42. World Scientific Press.

Dasgupta, S., and G. Mustafa. 2018. "Will Availability of Fish Decline in Sundarbans with Climate Change?" (blog) (in Bengali). https://blogs.worldbank.org/node/25397.

Dasgupta, S., M. G. Mustafa, T. Paul, and D. Wheeler. 2017b. "The Socioeconomics of Fish Consumption and Child Health: An Observational Cohort Study in Bangladesh." Policy Research Working Paper 8217, World Bank Group, Washington, DC.

Dasgupta, S., I. Sobhan, and D. Wheeler. 2017. "The Impact of Climate Change and Aquatic Salinization on Mangrove Species in the Bangladesh Sundarbans." *Ambio* 46 (6): 680–94.

Dasgupta, S., and D. Wheeler. 2018. "The Cyclone's Shadow: Historical Storm Impacts and Population Displacement in Bangladesh, West Bengal and Odisha." Paper prepared for the Sundarbans Targeted Environmental Studies, South Asia Water Initiative, World Bank, Washington, DC.

Dasgupta, S., and D. Wheeler. 2019a. "Accounting for Regional Differences in Mother and Child Health: Bangladesh, West Bengal, Bihar, and Jharkhand." Policy Research Working Paper 8798, World Bank Group, Washington, DC.

Dasgupta, S., and D. Wheeler. 2019b. "Explaining Regional Variations in Mother-Child Health: Environmental Determinants in India and Bangladesh." Paper prepared for the Sundarbans Targeted Environmental Studies, South Asia Water Initiative, World Bank, Washington, DC.

Development Initiatives. 2018. *2018 Global Nutrition Report: Shining a Light to Spur Action on Nutrition*. Bristol, UK: Development Initiatives.

FAO and WHO (Food and Agriculture Organization of the United Nations and World Health Organization). 2004. *Vitamin and Mineral Requirements in Human Nutrition: Report of a Joint FAO/WHO Expert Consultation*. 2nd ed. Geneva: World Health Organization.

Gain, A. K., M. N. Uddin, and P. Sana. 2008. "Impact of River Salinity on Fish Diversity in the South-West Coastal Region of Bangladesh." *International Journal of Ecology and Environmental Sciences* 34 (1): 49–54.

Hallenbeck, W. H., G. R. Brenniman, and R. J. Anderson. 1981. "High Sodium in Drinking Water and Its Effect on Blood Pressure." *American Journal of Epidemiology* 114: 817–26.

He, F. J., and G. A. MacGregor. 2007. "Salt, Blood Pressure and Cardiovascular Disease." *Current Opinion in Cardiology* 22: 298–305.

Joseph, G., Q. Wang, G. Chellaraj, M. Shamsudduha, and A. M. Naser. 2019. "Impact of Salinity on Infant and Neonatal Mortality in Bangladesh." Policy Research Working Paper 9058, World Bank, Washington, DC.

Kalaivani, K., and P. Ramachandran. 2018. "Time Trends in Prevalence of Anaemia in Pregnancy." *Indian Journal of Medical Research* 147 (3): 268–77.

Kawarazuka, N., and C. Bene. 2011. "The Potential Role of Small Fish Species in Improving Micronutrient Deficiencies in Developing Countries: Building Evidence." *Public Health and Nutrition* 14 (11): 1927–38.

Kent, G. 1987. *Fish, Food and Hunger: The Potential of Fisheries for Alleviating Malnutrition*. Boulder, CO: Westview Press.

Khan, A., S. K. Mojumder, S. Kovats, and P. Vineis. 2008. "Saline Contamination of Drinking Water in Bangladesh." *Lancet* 371 (9610): 385.

Khan, A., A. Ireson, S. Kovats, S. K. Mojumder, A. Khusru, A. Rahman, and P. Vineis. 2011. "Drinking Water Salinity and Maternal Health in Coastal Bangladesh: Implications of Climate Change." *Environmental Health Perspectives* 119 (9): 1328–32.

Michaelsen, K. F., K. G. Dewey, A. B. Perez-Exposito, M. Nurhasan, L. Lauritzen, and N. Roos. 2011. "Food Sources and Intake of n-6 and n-3 Fatty Acids in Low-income Countries with Emphasis on Infants, Young Children (6–24 months), and Pregnant and Lactating Women." *Maternal and Child Nutrition* 7: 124–40.

Midgley, J. P., A. G. Matthew, C. M. Greenwood, and A. G. Logan. 1996. "Effect of Reduced Dietary Sodium on Blood Pressure: A Meta-analysis of Randomized Controlled Trials." *Journal of the American Medical Association* 275: 1590–97.

Murphy, S. P., and L. H. Allen. 2003. "Nutritional Importance of Animal Source Foods." *Journal of Nutrition* 133 (11): 3932S–5S.

Naser, A., M. Rahman, L. Unicomb, S. Doza, M. S. Gazi, G. R. Alam, M. R. Karim, M. N. Uddin, G. K. Khan, K. M. Ahmed, and M. Shamsudduha. 2019. "Drinking Water Salinity, Urinary Macro-Mineral Excretions, and Blood Pressure in the Southwest Coastal Population of Bangladesh." *Journal of the American Heart Association* 8 (9): e012007.

Roos, N., M. Islam, and S. H. Thilsted. 2003. "Small Indigenous Fish Species in Bangladesh: Contribution to Vitamin A, Calcium and Iron Intakes." *Journal of Nutrition* 133 (11): 4021S–6S.

Scheelbeek, P., A. Khan, S. Mojumder, P. Elliott, and P. Vineis. 2016. "Drinking Water Sodium and Elevated Blood Pressure of Healthy Pregnant Women in Salinity-Affected Coastal Areas." *Hypertension* 68 (2): 464–70.

Toufique, K. A., and B. Belton. 2014. "Is Aquaculture Pro-Poor? Empirical Evidence of Impacts on Fish Consumption in Bangladesh." *World Development* 64: 609–20.

Vineis, P., Q. Chan, and A. Khan. 2011. "Climate Change Impacts on Water Salinity and Health." *Journal of Epidemiology and Global Health* 1 (1): 5–10.

Welty, T. K., L. Freni-Titulaer, M. M. Zack, P. Weber, J. Sippel, N. Huete, J. Justice, D. Dever, and M. A. Murphy. 1986. "Effects of Exposure to Salty Drinking Water in an Arizona Community: Cardiovascular Mortality, Hypertension Prevalence, and Relationships between Blood Pressure and Sodium Intake." *Journal of the American Medical Association* 255 (5): 622–26.

Wheal, M. S., E. DeCourcy-Ireland, J. R. Bogard, S. H. Thilsted, and J. C. Stangoulis. 2016. "Measurement of Haem and Total Iron in Fish, Shrimp and Prawn Using ICP-MS: Implications for Dietary Iron Intake Calculations." *Food Chemistry* 201: 222–29.

Wheeler, D., S. Dasgupta, T. Paul, and G. Mustafa. 2017. "May Our Children Always Have Fish and Rice!" (blog) (in Bengali). https://blogs.worldbank.org/node/25438.

4 Coping with Climate Change Vulnerability

INTRODUCTION

Proactive, climate-smart adaptation is required for poverty reduction and sustainable development in the Sundarbans (O'Donnell and Wodon 2015; Raha et al. 2013). Based on field investigations, this analytical study identified numerous adaptation measures appropriate for addressing the vulnerabilities of the poverty-stricken population in the Sundarbans Impact Zone of Bangladesh in a changing climate. The recommended measures, presented in three technical reports and journal articles (annex 4A), aim to reduce exposure of the poor to disasters, promote eco-friendly livelihood options, and protect the current and future stock of physical assets from salinization.

MEASURES TO REDUCE STORM-SURGE EXPOSURE

Embankment upgrading

Over the past half-century, the development of embankments, cyclone shelters, and early-warning and evacuation systems has dramatically reduced mortality from cyclone impacts (photo 4.1). However, reducing exposure of the vulnerable population to cyclones requires further improvements (figure 4.1). These include embankment reconstruction, rehabilitation, and realignment and height enhancement, along with construction of many more cyclone shelters that pay particular attention to enhanced access and sanitation facilities and improved emergency warning systems.[1]

Mangrove afforestation

The idea that healthy mangroves will reduce damage to adjacent coastal lands from cyclonic storm surges is well known in tropical coastal ecology and increasingly by coastal managers (Chapman 1976; Doney et al. 2012; Waite et al. 2014; Wells, Ravilious, and Corcoran 2006). As a surge moves through a mangrove

PHOTO 4.1

Coastal embankment in Dacope, Khulna

Source: © Md. Istiak Sobhan / World Bank. Further permission required for reuse.

FIGURE 4.1

Upgrading of embankments

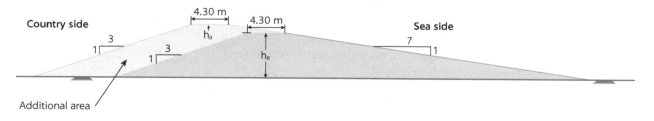

a. Sea-facing polders

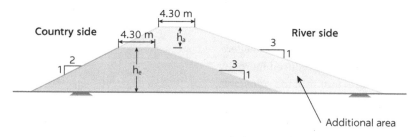

b. River-facing polders

Source: Dasgupta et al. 2010.
Note: h_a = the increment in height required to adapt to climate change; h_e = the current height of the embankment; m = meter.

forest, it faces obstruction from tree roots, trunks, and leaves. Damage is mitigated mainly through reduction in (1) surge height, which determines the area and depth of inundation, and (2) water-flow velocity. However, the extent of protection by mangroves depends strongly on an array of forest and location characteristics, which include density of tree plantings, diameter of trunks and roots, floor shape, and bathymetry, as well as spectral features of waves and the tidal stage at which waves enter the forest. Thus, the efficient use of this ecosystem-based protection often requires location-specific information on the protective capacity of mangroves (photo 4.2).

PHOTO 4.2

Mangrove trees

Source: © Pritthijit (Raja) Kundu. Reproduced with permission from Pritthijit (Raja) Kundu; further permission reqjuired for reuse.

FIGURE 4.2

Reduction in surge height from mangrove afforestation

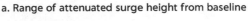

a. Range of attenuated surge height from baseline

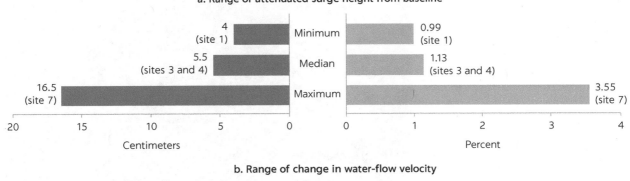

b. Range of change in water-flow velocity

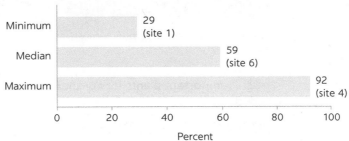

Source: Dasgupta et al. 2019.
Note: This study evaluated the protective capacity of five commonly found mangrove species at seven sites in Bangladesh where surge heights can reach up to 4 meters.

The hydrodynamic analysis conducted for this study evaluated the protective capacity of five commonly found mangrove species at seven sites in the cyclone-prone Sundarbans, where surge heights can reach 1.5–4 m (figure 4.2).[2] The research results showed that mangroves must be used with embankments and other built infrastructure to protect against risk

(Dasgupta 2019; Dasgupta and Blankespoor 2019). Through significant reduction in water-flow velocity, healthy mangroves on the foreshore of embankments will contribute to savings in rehabilitation and maintenance costs by protecting the built infrastructure from breaching, toe erosion, and other types of damage (Dasgupta 2017).

For optimum surge mitigation for polders 35/1, 40/1, and 40/2, which are currently under the Coastal Embankment Improvement Project, the study identified *Sonneratia apetala* and *Avicennia officinalis*, along with location-specific width and density of plantings. It was also pointed out that *S. apetala*, *Ceriops decandra*, and *Aeigicerus corniculatum*, when planted, will also enhance the potential for honey production (photo 4.3, table 4.1, and photo 4.4) (Dasgupta et al. 2020). This suggests that local people in the surrounding area could be involved in the co-management and maintenance of the mangrove trees and embankments.

PHOTO 4.3

Hive of *Apis dorsata* bees in Hingalganj, North 24 Parganas

Source: © Ajanta Dey. Reproduced with permission from Ajanta Dey; further permission required for reuse.

TABLE 4.1 **Important plants for apiculture: Nectar source and flowering period**

VERNACULAR NAME	BOTANICAL NAME	FLOWERING TIME
Khalsi	*Aegiceras corniculatum*	March–April
Goran	*Ceriops decandra*	April–May
Keora	*Sonneratia apetala*	End April–Mid-May
Passur	*Xylocarpus mekongensis*	End March–Mid-April
Genwa	*Excoecaria agallocha*	May–June
Kankra	*Bruguiera gymnorrhiza*	April
Baen	*Avicennia officinalis*	May–June

Source: Huq and Dasgupta 2018.

PHOTO 4.4
Apiculture in Gosaba, South 24 Parganas

Source: © Santadas Ghosh. Reproduced with permission from Santadas Ghosh; further permission required for reuse.

PHOTO 4.5
Multipurpose cyclone shelter in Dacope, Khulna

Source: © Md. Istiak Sobhan / World Bank. Further permission required for reuse.

Brick houses

This study also pointed out that, during emergencies, brick houses can serve as cyclone shelters of last resort, particularly if they are built on stilts, which would complement the large-capacity, multipurpose cyclone shelters currently being built by the Bangladesh government in collaboration with the World Bank and Asian Development Bank (photo 4.5). Future brick construction can be encouraged through appropriate subsidies and tax breaks for building materials, as well as subsidized loans for house construction.

Early-warning and evacuation systems

The current early-warning system for cyclones in the region is not specific to small areas, and does not give area-specific inundation-depth warnings. Significant gains can be realized by increasing the technical forecasting capacity of the Bangladesh Meteorological Department (BMD). Improvement will require an innovative compensation strategy since current BMD wages, which are tied to general government levels, are insufficient to attract employees with the requisite knowledge and skills.

Migration

Migration can bring opportunities for coping with climate change (Black et al. 2011; McLeman and Smit 2006). Analysis of data from the Bangladesh Demographic Health Survey indicates that out-migration among working-age adults in coastal-area households facing high inundation and salinization threats is already significantly higher than for their counterparts in nonthreatened areas (Dasgupta et al. 2016). However, human mobility from poor areas also has its challenges. For example, it often increases poverty among vulnerable family members left behind. Promoting voluntary out-migration to reduce coastal exposure and ecological pressure, while concurrently ensuring poverty alleviation of those remaining will require enhanced incentives. At the same time, innovative measures will be needed to prevent extremely poor residents from other areas from migrating to newly available land.

Focus group discussions with local experts and stakeholders in the Bangladesh Sundarbans Impact Zone indicated that enhanced literacy and skills training for local youth can contribute by enhancing opportunities for employment in urban export-oriented sectors. Training for drivers and mechanics can address rapidly growing demand in both the transport and transportation sectors. Training for garment production may be particularly attractive for women, who constitute the majority of garment-sector workers. Investment in such training should increase whole-family migration by providing economic incentives for wives to join their husbands in urban employment. Additional out-migration incentives can be provided by training for foreign employment, particularly in skills related to construction work, agriculture, cleaning, maintenance, and food-sector services. Appropriate training facilities can assist with job placement, as well as providing small loans to finance relocation.

MEASURES TO PROMOTE ECO-FRIENDLY LIVELIHOODS

Agriculture

The majority of people living in the Sundarbans Impact Zone identify agriculture as their primary occupation. Apart from own-labor, the sector also employs landless labor in the process of cultivation. Therefore, measures that promote climate adaptation in this sector will also contribute significantly to poverty reduction. Extension services should be provided for production of

PHOTO 4.6
Sunflower cultivation in the Sundarbans

Source: © Pritthijit (Raja) Kundu. Reproduced with permission from Pritthijit (Raja) Kundu; further permission required for reuse.

saline-resistant crops, along with promotion of wheat, maize (corn), sunflower, and other crops that are less water-intensive than Boro rice (the dominant crop). These services should also provide useful information and promote quality inputs for the homestead food production system, which plays an important nutritional role and is a good source of supplementary income for the rural poor, especially the functionally landless. The same applies to commercial apiculture, which may assume new importance as rising salinity shifts the mangrove stock toward species with greater potential for honey production.

Sunflower cultivation can play an important role in the socioeconomic development of the region (photo 4.6). There is significant demand for edible oil around the globe; thus, increased employment and income from sunflower farming can be achieved if effective business chains can be developed.

Fisheries expansion

Fish are a critical component of Bangladeshi diets, but fisheries management is poorly developed. Urgent priorities include developing a baseline assessment of fish stocks in the Sundarbans and assisting local fishing households to transition to new saline-tolerant species that can withstand rising water salinity as climate change proceeds.

One promising initiative is community based fisheries management, whereby community-based organizations are formed and exclusive fishing rights in relevant public water bodies are transferred to them. Assessment of local conditions indicates that the best results may be gained by focusing on the Sundarbans East Forest Division. Appropriate programs should ensure local ecological sustainability, as well as preservation of core fish stocks (photo 4.7). Expanded homestead pond aquaculture and cage aquaculture can also play significant roles in this context. Both activities can be enhanced by appropriate technical assistance and microcredit.

Prawn postlarvae catching with box nets

Source: © Md. Istiak Sobhan / World Bank. Further permission required for reuse.

Mud-crab aquaculture in the Sundarbans

Source: © Shushilan Reproduced with permission from Shushilan; further permission required for reuse.

Crab aquaculture opportunities

Mud-crab production can offer quite attractive returns in the Sundarbans coastal area (photo 4.8), but reliance on natural seed stocks must be reduced. To this end, Bangladesh should finance learning from established crab

PHOTO 4.9
Tourism in the Sundarbans

Source: © Pritthijit (Raja) Kundu. Reproduced with permission from Pritthijit (Raja) Kundu; further permission required for reuse.

producers (for example, China, India, Japan, and Vietnam). Some government assistance with appropriate hatchery siting may also be warranted. Evidence from West Bengal suggests that expansion of this sector will have a beneficial impact on women's employment. Expanded crab production will also encourage workers to move away from collecting prawn postlarvae (PPL) in the Sundarbans Reserve Forest and adjacent areas, which will reduce the adverse environmental and health impacts of this activity.

Tourism

The Sundarbans is a strong ecotourism destination, given that it constitutes the world's largest contiguous mangrove forest and is inhabited by the Royal Bengal Tiger (photo 4.9). Promotion of sustainable ecotourism should focus on activities that will directly benefit the local population. An appropriate program will also enhance tourists' knowledge of the Sundarbans, thereby increasing international support for conservation in the area. Promotion should include upgrading access infrastructure where needed, along with more extensive posting of relevant information and identification of local ceremonies and livelihoods that may be of particular interest to ecotourists. Local incomes can be enhanced by training residents as guides and promoting homestays for paying guests. To promote sustainability, ecotourism businesses should be held responsible for appropriate sustainability practices in their areas of operation.

INFRASTRUCTURE STRATEGIES TO PROTECT FROM SALINIZATION

Access to nonsaline drinking water

Inhabitants of the Sundarbans region suffer from water scarcity, resulting from elevated salinity during the dry season. Seeking access to nearby potable water becomes quite time-intensive during the dry season, particularly for women, and commercial sources can be too expensive for the poor. Promising initiatives in

PHOTO 4.10

Pond sand filter in Bhatiaghata, Khulna

Source: © Asif Zaman. Reproduced with permission from Asif Zaman; further permission required for reuse.

this sector include assistance with installation of rainwater harvesting systems, small local desalinization plants, and deep tube wells in areas where potable water can only be accessed from deep aquifers (photo 4.10).

Saline-resistant infrastructure

With rising family incomes in the coming decades, it is expected that the number of brick buildings with concrete roofs will increase sharply. Progressive salinity will mean a substantial increase in maintenance costs for these structures unless appropriate construction techniques are used. Acquiring and widely disseminating relevant information should be priority measures for public authorities. Similar considerations apply to road infrastructure, but appropriate investment in this sector is complicated by the risk that improved roads will draw migrants to climate-vulnerable areas while increasing pressure on fragile ecosystems. For such areas, appropriate policies should include encouragement of nonmotorized traffic; preventing the paving of roads near forest areas; and implementing measures to counteract salinity-damage risks in areas where road improvement is warranted.

Need for locally oriented collective action

Cost-effective adaptation to climate-related changes in the Sundarbans will require local support for appropriate collective action, combined with increased public investment. For example, a large proportion of the millions of Bangladeshis who currently own smartphones live in rural areas. Dissemination of relevant information via smartphones could include more accurate and

"This program of research on the panoply of challenges in the Sundarbans from climate change starkly illustrates that without strong counter-measures, people will confront threats to economic productivity and poverty alleviation through a variety of channels, including elevated health risks, reduced land and labor productivity, degradation of natural ecosystems, greater exposure to extreme events, and higher infrastructure investment costs. Fortunately, the research also shows that much of the needed response may be accomplished at relatively modest cost through resilience-smart development policies and investments."

—Michael Toman, research manager, Development Economics Research Group, World Bank

timely weather alerts, practical-information and skills-development videos (for example, through YouTube), and easily accessible websites in the Bangla language. To be effective, however, collective action requires that problems across the affected population be similarly perceived. The survey conducted by this study team in the Indian Sundarbans shows that perceptions of environmental problems vary significantly across localities. Even within localities, perceptions differ by household, especially among elite households. Effective management of environmental resources in the Sundarbans will require locally oriented collective action with local governance that promotes nonelite participation (Dasgupta, Guha, and Wheeler 2020).[3]

ANNEX 4A: RELEVANT PUBLICATIONS

This annex lists the publications produced under the analytical program that are relevant to coping with the vulnerability of the Sundarbans in a changing climate.

Technical reports and journal articles

Co-Location, Socioeconomic Status and Perceptions of Environmental Change in the Indian Sundarbans, https://ecoinsee.org/journal/papers/issue-3-1/76.pdf.

Quantifying the Protective Capacity of Mangroves from Storm Surges in Bangladesh, https://journals.plos.org/plosone/article?id=10.1371/journal.pone.0214079.

The Sundarbans: Climate Change and Adaptation Measures, http://www.sundarbansonline.org/wp-content/uploads/2020/03/Paper-Climate-Change-and-Adaptation-Measures-for-Bangladesh-Sundarban.pdf.

Web feature stories

Can Mangroves Mitigate Catastrophic Consequences of Cyclone-Induced Storm Surges?, https://www.preventionweb.net/news/view/64752.

Mangroves and Coastal Protection: A Potential Triple-Win for Bangladesh, https://blogs.worldbank.org/endpovertyinsouthasia/mangroves-and-coastal-protection-potential-triple-win-bangladesh?CID=WBW_AL_BlogNotification_EN_EXT.

Protection from Cyclones: Benefits of Integrating Green and Gray Infrastructure, http://blogs.worldbank.org/developmenttalk/protection-cyclones-benefits -integrating-green-and-gray-infrastructure.

When Cyclones Strike: Using Mangroves to Protect Coastal Areas, https:// blogs.worldbank.org/developmenttalk/when-cyclones-strike-using-mangroves -protect-coastal-areas.

NOTES

1. In the early 1960s and 1970s, 143 polders, including 49 sea-facing ones, were built in coastal Bangladesh to protect agricultural land from tidal flooding and salinity intrusion. Currently, the Bangladesh government is undertaking the reconstruction, rehabilitation, and realignment and height enhancement of a few of these polders in the cyclone-prone Sundarbans Impact Zone to reduce the storm-surge exposure of local inhabitants.

2. At each site, measurements of the root and trunk systems of the relevant mangrove species and spacing between trees were undertaken to estimate Manning's coefficients. A hydro-dynamic model for the Bay of Bengal, based on the MIKE21FM modeling system, was set up, calibrated, and run multiple times to simulate the surge of Cyclone Sidr, which made landfall in the Bangladesh Sundarbans in 2007 with a maximum wind speed of 248 kph, maximum wind radius of 64 km, central pressure of 928 hPa, and normal pressure of 1,009 hPa. Estimates of surge height and water-flow velocity were first recorded without mangroves and then with differing widths of mangrove forests under various planting densities using specific information on local topography, bathymetry, and Manning coefficients estimated from the root and trunk systems of relevant mangrove species. Results showed varying levels of protection from mangroves, depending on the selected species, forest width, and planting density. Overall, estimates indicated a modest reduction in surge height, in a range of 4–16.5 cm, and a significant reduction in water-flow velocity, at 29–92 percent. *Sonneratia apetala* was found to cause maximum obstruction to surge water, followed by *Avicennia officinalis* and *Heritiera fomes*. Maximum reduction in water-flow velocity was recorded for a 50 m wide belt of *S. apetala* at 5 m spacing in sea-facing areas.

3. These findings are from a regression analysis conducted by this analytical program with new survey data, which explored variations in environmental perceptions across classes and localities in the Indian Sundarbans. The analysis comprised 600 households in Dwarir Jangle, Sandeshkhali II Block in North 24–Parganas District and Kumirmari, Gosaba Block, Kankandighi, Mathurapur II Block in South 24–Parganas District.

REFERENCES

Black, R., S. R. Bennett, S. M. Thomas, and J. R. Beddington. 2011. "Migration as Adaptation." *Nature* 478 (7370): 447–49.

Chapman, V. J. 1976. *Mangrove Vegetation*. Vaduz, Liechtenstein: Cramer.

Dasgupta, S. 2017. "When Cyclones Strike: Using Mangroves to Protect Coastal Areas." *Let's Talk Development* (blog), November 28. World Bank, Washington DC. https://blogs .worldbank.org/developmenttalk/when-cyclones-strike-usingmangrovesprotect -coastal-areas.

Dasgupta, S. 2019. "Can Mangroves Mitigate Catastrophic Consequences of Cyclone-Induced Storm Surges?" *Prevention Web*. https://www.preventionweb.net/news/view/64752.

Dasgupta, S., and B. Blankespoor. 2019. "Protection from Cyclones: Benefits of Integrating Green and Gray Infrastructure." *Prevention Web*. https://www.preventionweb.net/news /view/64719.

Dasgupta, S., B. Guha, and D. Wheeler. 2020. "Co-Location, Socioeconomic Status and Perceptions of Environmental Change in the Indian Sundarbans." *Ecology, Economy and Society—The INSEE Journal* 3 (1): 47–67. https://doi.org/10.37773/ees.v3i1.88.

Dasgupta, S., M. Hossain, M. Huq, and D. Wheeler. 2016. "Facing the Hungry Tide: Climate Change, Livelihood Threats and Household Responses in Coastal Bangladesh." *Climate Change Economics* 7 (3): 1–25.

Dasgupta, S., M. Huq, Z. H. Khan, M. Z. Ahmed, N. Mukherjee, M. F. Khan, and K. Pandey. 2010. "Vulnerability of Bangladesh to Cyclones in a Changing Climate: Potential Damages and Adaptation Cost." Policy Research Working Paper 5280, World Bank, Washington, DC.

Dasgupta, S., M. S. Islam, M. Huq, Z. H. Khan, and M. R. Hasib. 2019. "Quantifying the Protective Capacity of Mangroves from Storm Surges in Coastal Bangladesh." *PLoS One* 14 (3): e0214079. http://doi.org/10.1371/journalpone.0214079.

Dasgupta, S., M. I. Sobhan, M. Huq, and Z. H. Khan. 2020. "Mangroves and Coastal Protection: A Potential Triple-Win for Bangladesh." *End Poverty in South Asia* (blog), July 16. World Bank, Washington, DC. https://blogs.worldbank.org/endpovertyinsouthasia/mangroves -and-coastal-protection-potential-triple-win-bangladesh.

Doney, S. C., M. Ruckelshaus, J. E. Duffy, J. P. Barry, F. Chan, C. A. English, H. M. Galindo, J. M. Grebmeier, A. B. Hollowed, N. Knowlton, J. Polovina, N. Rabalais, W. Sydeman, and L. Talley. 2012. "Climate Change Impacts on Marine Ecosystems." *Annual Review of Marine Science* 4: 11–37.

Huq, M., and S. Dasgupta. 2018. "The Sundarbans: Climate Change and Adaptation Measures." Paper prepared for the Sundarbans Targeted Environmental Studies, South Asia Water Initiative, World Bank, Washington, DC.

McLeman, R., and B. Smit. 2006. "Migration as an Adaptation to Climate Change." *Climatic Change* 76 (1–2): 31–53.

O'Donnell, A., and Q. Wodon, eds. 2015. *Climate Change Adaptation and Social Resilience in the Sundarbans*. London: Routledge.

Raha, A. K., S. Zaman, K. Sengupta, S. B. Bhattacharyya, S. Raha, K. Banerjee, and A. Mitra. 2013. "Climate Change and Sustainable Livelihood Programme: A Case Study from Indian Sundarbans." *Journal of Ecology* 107 (6): 335–48.

Waite, R., L. Burke, E. Gray, P. van Beukering, L. Brander, E. Mackenzie, L. Pendleton, P. Schuhmann, and E. L. Tompkins. 2014. *Coastal Capital: Ecosystem Valuation for Decision Making in the Caribbean*. Washington, DC: World Resources Institute.

Wells, S., C. Ravilious, and E. Corcoran. 2006. *In the Front Line: Shoreline Protection and Other Ecosystem Services from Mangroves and Coral Reefs*. Biodiversity Series 24. Cambridge, UK: United Nations Environment Programme World Conservation Monitoring Centre.

5 Lessons in Reducing Climate Change Vulnerability

INTRODUCTION

This chapter summarizes what was learned from the multidisciplinary technical studies conducted for the Sundarbans region under the analytical program described in this book. The chapter begins by summarizing the key impacts of climate change on the Sundarbans ecosystem and its local inhabitants, followed by suggested adaptation measures. Next, it describes opportunities for applying the key findings from the analytical program's studies to coastal resilience projects. It then turns to the broader program lessons for developing more effective projects. Finally, key lessons from the analytical program's collaborative process for assessing climate change vulnerability are presented.

ECOSYSTEM IMPACTS

Understanding the Sundarbans from a historical perspective is critical for assessing the ecosystem's vulnerability in a changing climate. Setting baselines using historical data is an essential prerequisite.

- For this analytical exercise, the assembling of baselines developed from older maps, satellite images, and data from official archives indicated that, irrespective of climate change, the Sundarban islands are undergoing erosion, and this trend holds true whether the Indian and Bangladesh Sundarbans are considered separately or together. For some islands, the rate of linear coastline retreat is as high as 40 m per year, meaning they face complete obliteration within the next 50–100 years.
- Despite pronounced period-to-period shifts, the median location of cyclones has shifted eastward over time. Currently, the Indian Sundarbans is the highest impact zone for tropical cyclones in the Bay of Bengal.[1]

Climate change has already affected the Sundarbans ecosystem significantly. Its future impacts will differ substantially across the region's complex landscape in magnitude and time-phasing, creating differential transboundary pressures for adaptation and relocation of both human communities and endangered species. Unless the responsible agencies in India and Bangladesh are equipped to promote climate resilience, with knowledge of the affected communities and ecosystems, future changes may undermine regional management.

- Sea-level rise is a major threat. In a changing climate, it is expected that the Sundarbans landscape will undergo significant fragmentation, causing habitat loss for many endangered species. If resource scarcity necessitates prioritizing areas of unique flora and fauna for conservation, then the core region, which has high species vulnerability and where inundation in this century is least likely, should be assigned the highest-priority status.[2]
- Progressive salinization of water and soil will result in greater dominance of salt-tolerant mangrove species at the expense of freshwater species. By 2050, significant overall losses will occur for *Heritiera fomes*, with substantial gains for *Avicennia*, *Excoecaria*, and *Ceriops* sp., as well as species assemblages with medium-to-high salt tolerance. Salinity-induced mangrove migration will have a strongly regressive impact on the value of timber stocks in the Sundarbans core forest due to the loss of *Heretiera fomes*—the highest-value timber species.
- Habitats for freshwater fish will also shrink. The predicted changes for 2012–50 indicate that brackish-water habitats will expand moderately into the freshwater habitat of the Bangladesh Sundarbans. Due to habitat loss, many small, indigenous freshwater species in the wild (for example, *Eutropiichthys vacha, Cirrhinus reba, Chela laubuca, Mystus vittatus, Ailia coila, Cynoglossus lingua,* and *Salmostoma bacalia*) will be threatened or even become regionally extinct.[3]

POPULATION IMPACTS

With sea-level rise and progressive salinization, the Sundarbans region will face significant changes in the quality of water and soil, as well as alterations in flora and fauna. Many parts of the region will reach near ocean-level salinity (32 ppt) by 2050, which is likely to cause shortages in drinking water, water scarcity for dry-season irrigation, and significant changes in coastal aquatic ecosystems in the core forest and reclaimed areas.[4] It is expected that the lives and livelihoods of poor households, including the region's most vulnerable population segments (that is, women, children, and the elderly) will be affected the most. The key impacts are highlighted below.

- Shortage in drinking water due to the salinization of rivers and groundwater will have significant implications for the time-activity patterns of households, especially during the dry season, with disproportionate effects on women, who must allocate more time to accessing potable water. As the salinity of drinking water increases, the impacts on mother-child health include dehydration, hypertension, prenatal complications, and increased infant mortality. Areas especially at risk include Bagerhat, Barguna, Khulna, and Pirojpur districts in Bangladesh's Sundarban Impact Zone and Hingalgunj Block in India's Sundarbans Reclaimed Region.
- The decline in freshwater fish species from progressive river salinization will adversely impact the livelihoods of many poor fishers in the Sundarbans Impact Zone. Any significant gain in brackish-water species is unlikely since

wild marine and brackish fish prefer coastal ecosystems to river systems due to their feeding habits and biology. This study identified five saline-tolerant fish species, comprising 31 percent of the current fish catch, that have the potential to thrive in aquaculture: *Mystus gulio, Pama pama, Liza parsia, Lates calcarifer,* and *Acantho paguslatus.*

- The stakes from declining freshwater fish species are especially high for mother-child health and nutrition. In Bangladesh, three upazilas (subdistricts) exhibiting the top 10 species-loss indicators are located in the Sundarbans Impact Zone: Bagerhat, Morrelganj, and Rampal. In this area, chronic and acute malnutrition levels for mothers and children are higher than the thresholds set by the World Health Organization (WHO) for public-health emergencies, as indicated by statistics on wasting and stunting of children and anemia among women of reproductive age. Thus, policies that promote fish consumption among poor households and programs that increase poor households' fish supply may significantly improve mother-child health.

- An analysis of regional variations in child wasting and maternal anemia for Bangladesh and the neighboring Indian states of West Bengal, Bihar, and Jharkhand indicates that regional and temporal variations in the water cycle through flood and drought conditions affect mother-child health as strongly as more commonly cited socioeconomic factors (for example, mother's education, mother's age, household wealth, and child birth order). Floods and droughts most likely affect mother-child health through their impacts on the price and availability of critical nutrients (for example, fish and other animal-source foods), environmental conditions, and family hygiene. The sensitivity of mother-child health to flood-proneness implies increased vulnerability as extreme weather events increase with climate change.

- Progressive river salinization will adversely impact the livelihoods, health, and safety of the rural poor. For example, women who engage in saline-immersive, prawn postlarvae (PPL) catching report far more health problems than their counterparts who engage in otherwise comparable, low-wage economic activities.[5] Forest-based livelihoods for poor households will also be adversely impacted by changes in the composition of mangrove species resulting from progressive water salinization. For example, it is expected that the reduced value of standing timber and honey production will have the greatest impact in Shyamnagar, the poorest upazila in the Bangladesh Sundarbans Impact Zone. Moreover, as the diversity of mangrove species diminishes, so could the region's attractiveness as a biodiversity destination.

- Fragmentation of the Sundarbans landscape will increase the loss of wildlife habitat (for example, for tigers and venomous snakes). This, in turn, is expected to increase the risk of human-wildlife conflicts in the region.

- Poor households that end up settling in low-lying areas close to the coast and creeks are disadvantaged by a lack of land access. Even though climate change puts their livelihoods at greater risk (that is, from increasing frequency and intensity of cyclone strikes, greater risk of tidal inundation, and progressive river salinization), they remain, owing to high land prices and a lack of employment opportunities elsewhere.

- In the Bangladesh Sundarbans, economic necessity is driving more (mainly male) working-age adults to seek outside earnings. But out-migration has also increased the poverty of the population left behind since it takes considerable time for low-skilled migrant family members to save sufficient funds to remit back home. By contrast, out-migration is still uncommon in the Indian

Sundarbans Reclaimed Region. It may be that India's extensive compensation programs have significantly dampened the responsiveness of population dynamics to climate-related locational disadvantages.

PROACTIVE ADAPTATION

Effective management of the Sundarbans requires knowledge of the ecosystem and the communities that depend on it, including an understanding of their current responses to the impacts of climate change and resilience planning that anticipates their future responses as climate change proceeds.

- Mangrove protection and restoration are urgently needed to reduce the damage of adjacent coastal lands from cyclonic storm surges. However, the protective capacity of mangroves varies, depending on tree species, forest width, and planting density. Among the species commonly found in the Sundarbans, *Sonneratia apetala* causes maximum obstruction to surge water, followed by *Avicennia officinalis* and *Heritiera fomes*.[6]
- In the densely populated, cyclone-prone reclaimed areas of the Sundarbans, where surge heights can reach 1.5–4.0 m, mangrove protection and restoration ("green" infrastructure) must be combined with strengthening built ("gray") infrastructure (for example, public cyclone shelters and embankments) to protect against inundation risk. Through significant reduction in water-flow velocity, healthy mangroves will contribute to significant savings in rehabilitation and maintenance costs by protecting the built infrastructure from breaching, toe erosion, and other types of damage. Healthy mangroves offer "win-win" adaptation measures since they also enhance livelihood opportunities. Additional critical elements include brick houses on stilts in every neighborhood as shelters of last resort and improved early-warning and disaster-forecasting systems for small areas.
- Options for additional infrastructure investment to protect from growing salinization include assistance with small-scale, local desalinization plants; rainwater harvesting; and precautionary measures taken before constructing buildings, roads, and other infrastructure.
- Field investigations identified numerous adaptation measures for reducing the exposure of vulnerable populations to cyclone disasters. These include training and skills development to strengthen the human capital and earning potential of the working-age population that is voluntarily out-migrating, enhancing eco-friendly livelihood options for the nonmigrating population, and developing infrastructure strategies as protection from salinization.[7] For the out-migrating population, the government should persuade institutes that it designates to put forward training programs in climate-vulnerable areas and provide eligible locals with redeemable coupons usable only for those training programs. For the nonmigrating population, suggested areas of training include commercial driving for men, textile-factory work for women, construction work, and cleaning and food-sector services (for foreign employment), along with job-placement services and provision of loans for financing relocation. Microenterprise start-up financing or training is also needed to assist the nonmigrating population in pursuing or enhancing eco-friendly livelihoods (for example, sunflower cultivation, mud-crab culture, homestead pond aquaculture, community-based fisheries management, commercial apiculture, and nature-based tourism).

INFORMING COASTAL RESILIENCE PROJECTS

Many of the lessons from the multidisciplinary technical studies conducted under this analytical program can be applied to various ongoing and proposed coastal resilience projects in Bangladesh and India. For example, the studies' findings on geomorphological changes (erosion and accretion) in the Sundarban islands, changing cyclonic patterns and population dynamics, and estimates of the protective capacity of mangrove species are especially useful for the Integrated Coastal Zone Management projects, Cyclone Risk Mitigation projects, Coastal Embankment improvement projects, and Multipurpose Disaster Shelter projects. The study findings on the changing composition of mangroves and fish availability are useful for projects seeking to develop integrated, eco-friendly measures to protect resource-dependent households and communities against the adverse impacts of climate change; these include Sustainable Forest and Livelihood projects, Sustainable Coastal and Marine Fisheries projects, and the Blue Economy and Sundarbans Assessment in Bangladesh and India.

Specific findings from the analytical program's technical studies have also informed particular World Bank–supported projects, as follows:

- Quantification of potential habitat loss of freshwater fish species and habitat gain of brackish-water fish species with progressive water salinization and identification of fish species (*Mystus gulio, Pama pama, Liza parsia, Lates calcarifer,* and *Acantho paguslatus*) with the potential to thrive in aquaculture informed preparation of the Bangladesh Sustainable Coastal and Marine Fisheries Project and the Bangladesh Blue Economy and Sundarbans Assessment.
- Quantification of salinity-tolerance thresholds of mangrove species commonly found in the Sundarbans and maps of likely migration of mangrove species with progressive water salinization in a changing climate informed the Sustainable Forest and Livelihood Project in Bangladesh.
- Estimation of varying levels of reductions in storm-surge height and water-flow velocity from various species of mangroves, as well as alternative width and density of mangrove forests, were used to inform the mangrove afforestation components for Polders 35/1, 40/1, and 40/2 under the Bangladesh Coastal Embankment Improvement Project.[8]

Beyond informing current and proposed resilience projects, the usefulness of the study findings and lessons can be extended to help identify new climate-resilience projects for the Sundarbans and fragile coastal regions elsewhere.

"The findings from this World Bank research will immediately help in designing the forest cover in the foreshore of polders to attenuate storm surge and wave and water velocity during cyclones and complement the height of embankments as part of the coastal protection infrastructure."

—Zahirul Huque Khan, director, Coast, Port and Estuary Division, Institute of Water Modelling and advisor, Coastal Embankment Improvement Project, Dhaka

BROADER LESSONS FOR ASSESSING CLIMATE CHANGE VULNERABILITY

Among the broader program lessons that emerge from the analytical program, the following can be highlighted:

- *History matters.* Setting accurate technical baselines using historical data is an essential prerequisite for understanding the vulnerability of ecosystems and human communities in a changing climate. As part of this analytical exercise, information from older maps, satellite images, and data from official archives were assembled to develop such a baseline.
- *Local knowledge and analysis matter.* With sea-level rise and progressive salinization, the developing world's coastal regions will face significant changes in the quality of water and soil, as well as alterations in flora and fauna. It is expected that the lives and livelihoods of poor households, including the regions' most vulnerable population segments (women, children, and the elderly) will be affected the most. But climate impacts and their policy implications will be greatly affected by local socioeconomic, topographical, and environmental conditions. To be effective, policies must take these local considerations into account.
- *Local consultation matters.* Localized research cannot identify the key leverage points for effective policy interventions without understanding the insights, institutions, and incentives of the people who live in the affected areas.

Summing up, this analytical program finds that policies for assessing climate change vulnerability are far more effective when informed by area-specific knowledge and multidisciplinary analysis. Utilizing such a pragmatic approach to identify the impacts on resources, livelihoods, and health outcomes facilitates the development of more effective, context-specific measures for promoting adaptation.

KEY LESSONS FROM THE COLLABORATIVE PROCESS

The impacts of climate change on the Sundarbans ecosystem and local population are complex and multifaceted. Effective management of the region will require multidisciplinary collaboration among scientists and sharing technical expertise between Bangladesh and India, as well as knowledge sharing with other countries experiencing similar problems.

The key lessons from this collaborative process are as follows:

- Designing and implementing regional management protocols for the Sundarbans in a changing climate require close collaboration between hydrologists, soil scientists, ecologists, economists, engineers, and regional planners.
- Technical experts in both Bangladesh and India are willing and available to work together on management of the transboundary Sundarbans biosphere. Successful resilience planning between these neighboring countries requires a collaborative work arrangement that draws on their complementary skills. Working together is both feasible and effective for establishing a common understanding of shared challenges and a respectful discussion space in which to carry out resilience planning.

- Significant opportunities are available for knowledge sharing and information exchange between countries in the Bengal and Mekong deltas, many of which are facing similar challenges in a changing climate. Various countries in Asia with low-lying coastal regions have already expressed interest in learning from one another's successes and failures. The World Bank's convening capacity as a knowledge bank can facilitate this process.

NOTES

1. According to the Bangladesh Meteorological Department (BMD), India Meteorological Department (IMD), and Global Data Center for Meteorology.
2. According to BirdLife International, International Union for Conservation of Nature (IUCN), and World Wildlife Fund (WWF).
3. According to the World Bank River Salinity Information System and WorldFish.
4. According to the Bangladesh Institute of Water Modelling (IWM), WWF, NEWS, and field measurements conducted by this analytical program.
5. Generally older, less-educated women engage in this hazardous occupation. Appropriate policies can help by subsidizing healthier employment alternatives or developing catching techniques that reduce saline immersion time.
6. Maximum reduction in water velocity was recorded for a 50 m wide belt of *Sonneratia apetala* at 5 m spacing in sea-facing areas.
7. It should be noted that the recommendations of these studies are proposed specifically for the Sundarbans landscape region and are not necessarily applicable to any other rural areas of Bangladesh or India.
8. To maximize the mitigation in storm-surge height and water-flow velocity, the study recommended specific mangrove species and planting widths and densities. For Polder 35/1 (foreshore areas), 50 m *Sonneratia apetala* at 5 m spacing was recommended, followed by 50 m *Avicennia officinalis* at 6 m spacing. For Polder 40/1, 50 m *S. apetala* at 5 m spacing was recommended, followed by 50 m *A. officinalis* at 4 m spacing and 2,000 m *Ceriops decandra* at 5 m spacing. For Polder 40/2, 50 m *S. apetala* at 5 m spacing was recommended, followed by 50 m *A. officinalis* at 4 m spacing.

6 Institutional Capacity Building

INTRODUCTION

Prior to implementing this analytical program, the availability of data-intensive, multidisciplinary research on the transboundary Sundarbans was quite limited from a regional perspective. These studies addressed this gap by establishing technical cooperation between neighboring Bangladesh and India to conduct climate vulnerability analysis in the ecoregion. In the process, they strengthened their institutional capacity for conducting policy-relevant, multidisciplinary research—one of the main goals of this initiative.

TECHNICAL COOPERATION

The analytical program's multidisciplinary studies successfully established cooperation between researchers from Bangladesh and India and drew on their complementary skills to conduct collaborative empirical research in the Sundarbans. Older maps of the Sundarbans coastline predating the 1947 partition of India were shared to analyze the region's erosion and accretion over the past century. Data from the Bangladesh Meteorological Department (BMD) and the India Meteorological Department (IMD) were compiled and compared to develop a combined database of cyclone landfalls along the Sundarbans coastline from 1877 to 2016.

Hydrological models were used to project the impacts of climate change on the progressive salinization of water in the Bangladesh Sundarbans. The estimates extrapolated were then used to predict water salinity in the Indian Sundarbans, where data to support water-salinity modeling are inadequate. The impacts of progressive salinization on mangrove species and the forest-based livelihoods of poor populations in the surrounding area were first predicted for the Bangladesh Sundarbans. The Indian researchers learned about the study methodology from the Bangladeshi researchers and adapted it to predict changes in mangrove-species composition in the Indian Sundarbans.

"This research provided the government of Bangladesh with a spatio-temporal assessment of vulnerability, as well as a menu of feasible investment options. It contributed to five out of six pillars of the Climate Change Strategy and Action Plan of Bangladesh. This analytical approach can also be used as a tool for future research."

—Ainun Nishat, professor emeritus, BRAC University and principal member, Climate Change Negotiation Committee of Bangladesh

The Bangladeshi and Indian researchers developed common survey instruments (that is, questionnaires and a sampling strategy) and used them to collect primary data on the impacts of environmental degradation in the region on livelihoods, perceptions of climate change risk, and population dynamics. Experts from the two neighboring countries also worked together to analyze cross-regional variations in mother-child health outcomes using data from Bangladesh's Demographic and Health Survey. This exercise helped the researchers to develop an understanding of the potential underlying reasons for locational differences in health outcomes—which prior to this study were unexplained by determinants commonly cited in the literature—and the critical role of environmental factors. Technical cooperation between the two countries is ongoing. For example, the University of Calcutta and Khulna University recently signed a memorandum of understanding (MoU) for collaborative research on the Sundarbans, and study tours are taking place.

KNOWLEDGE EXCHANGE WORKSHOP

A highlight of this research collaboration was the knowledge exchange workshop, Vulnerability of the Sundarbans in a Changing Climate, which was held in Calcutta in February 2017 (photo 6.1).[1] The workshop brought together 400 researchers from Bangladesh and India seeking to better understand the physical and economic impacts of climate change on the Sundarbans. The first day of the workshop featured presentations of completed and ongoing technical studies from Bangladesh and India (photo 6.1a), while the second focused on hands-on training in modeling the physical impacts of climate change on the Sundarbans (photo 6.1b).

The workshop not only utilized multidisciplinary studies to assess the impact of climate change on the iconic Sundarbans landscape; it also facilitated the large-scale sharing of technical knowledge between the neighboring countries. This was a step forward in establishing a common data protocol and research methodology for bilateral management of the Sundarbans, including the integration of climate-related concerns into both countries' relevant plans and programs for sustainable ecosystem management and poverty alleviation in adjacent areas.

PHOTO 6.1
Knowledge exchange workshop

a. Presentations of technical studies

b. Training by the Institute of Water Modelling

Source: World Bank.

KNOWLEDGE SHARING BEYOND THE STUDY REGION

Worldwide, some 600 million people currently live in low-elevation coastal zones that will be affected by progressive salinization and inundation with sea-level rise in a changing climate. Recently published scientific reports suggest that sea level may rise by 1 m or more in the 21st century, which would increase the vulnerable population to about 1 billion. Families in the Sundarbans region are already on the front line of climate change. Their experience, behavior, and adaptation signal future decisions by hundreds of millions of families that will face similar threats by 2100. Thus, knowledge sharing opportunities between countries with low-lying deltaic areas are significant.

The strong interest in the study results by Asian countries in the Mekong Delta, which are facing similar challenges, stems from the program's unique status: This is the first cross-boundary study program that has shown how general climate-induced changes in weather patterns, hydrology, and salinity translate into location-specific impacts on coastal communities and ecosystems. Interest from Mekong Delta countries has focused particularly on the program's methodology for identifying effects on specific resources, livelihoods, and health outcomes. This pragmatic approach to research facilitates the identification of localized policy initiatives to address the increasing impacts of climate change. In response to the expressed interest of countries in the Mekong Delta region, the methodology and findings of the multidisciplinary research conducted under the analytical program were presented to the Lower Mekong Public Policy Initiative (LMPPI) team (photo 6.2) and Vietnam's Institute of Strategy and Policy on Natural Resources and Environment (annex 6A).

PHOTO 6.2

Sharing learning from the analytic program with the Lower Mekong Public Policy Initiative

Source: © Pritthijit (Raja) Kundu. Reproduced with permission from Pritthijit (Raja) Kundu; further permission required for reuse.
Note: The event took place in Ho Chi Minh City, Vietnam, on December 9, 2016.

PHOTO 6.3

Sharing learning from the analytical program with scholars at Southwestern University of Finance and Economics in China

Source: © Pritthijit (Raja) Kundu. Reproduced with permission from Pritthijit (Raja) Kundu; further permission required for reuse.
Note: The event took place in Chengdu, China, on November 29, 2016.

Broader interest in learning about multidisciplinary research on the Sundarbans led to presenting the analytical program's research methodology and findings to a wide variety of institutions in the Asia region (annex 6A). These included 24 universities spanning Bangladesh (5), China (8), India (8), Singapore (1), and Vietnam (2) (photo 6.3). Summary presentations of the findings were

"This initiative has set the stage for pursuing the climate change agenda in an intensive manner. This is the first step, a very important one. Now we need to discuss more on how these inputs can feed into framing [the] right policy framework."

—Prabhat K. Mishra, West Bengal Department of Fisheries, India

made at four professional conferences, including a keynote address delivered at the 9th Biennial Conference of the Indian Society for Ecological Economics in Kerala, and six World Bank–organized seminars. In addition, the methodology and findings were shared with the Asian Development Bank and several World Bank development-partner organizations, including the Australian Department of Foreign Affairs and Trade, the Norwegian Agency for Development Cooperation, the UK Department for International Development, and WorldFish, an international nongovernmental organization.

ANNEX 6A: LIST OF TRAINING SEMINARS

Bangladesh

Independent University, Dhaka, August 2016

Bangladesh University of Engineering and Technology, Dhaka, December 2017

BRAC University, Dhaka, December 2017

North South University, Dhaka, December 2017

University of Liberal Arts, Dhaka, December 2017

WorldFish, December 2017

Cambodia

WorldFish, November 2017

China

Beijing Normal University, Beijing, November 2016

Sichuan University, Chengdu, November 2016

Southwestern University of Finance and Economics, Chengdu, November 2016

Tsinghua University, Beijing, November 2016

Innovative Technology of Watershed Ecological Engineering and Environmental Management and 20th Anniversary of PACE Association, Beijing, August 2017

Chinese University of Hong Kong, Hong Kong SAR, China, November 2017

Hunan Normal University, Changsha, November 2017

Peking University, Beijing, November 2017

Renmin University, Beijing, November 2017

India

Center for Urban Studies, Calcutta, January 2016

Knowledge Exchange Seminar on Sundarbans, Calcutta, February 2017

University of Calcutta, Calcutta, May 2017

Indian Institute of Management, Calcutta, May 2017

Presidency University, Calcutta, May 2017

Keynote Address, 9th Biennial Conference of Indian Society for Ecological Economics, Thrissur, Kerala, November 2017

Jadavpur University, Calcutta, January 2018

Institute of Economic Growth, New Delhi, December 2018

TERI University, New Delhi, December 2018

Jawaharlal Nehru University, New Delhi, July 2019

South Asia Water Initiative Development Partners, New Delhi, August 2019

Philippines

Asian Development Bank, December 2017

Singapore

National University of Singapore, December 2017

Sweden

Sixth World Congress of Environmental and Resource Economists, Gothenburg, June 2018

Vietnam

Institute of Strategy and Policy on Natural Resources and Environment, Ministry of Natural Resources and Environment, Hanoi, December 2016

University of Economics, Ho Chi Minh City, December 2016

Lower Mekong Public Policy Initiative team, Ho Chi Minh City, December 2017

National Economics University, Hanoi, December 2017

World Bank offices

World Bank, Manila, December 2017

World Bank, Singapore, December 2017

World Bank, Dhaka, July 2019

World Bank, New Delhi, August 2019

World Bank headquarters, Washington, DC, January 2018

World Bank headquarters, Washington, DC, November 2019

NOTE

1. Details from the South Asia Water Initiative Knowledge Exchange Workshop (February 3–4, 2017) are available at sundarbansonline.org/wp-content/uploads/2020/06/Summary-SAWI -Workshop-Vulnerability-of-Sundarbans-in-a-Changing-Climate-February-2017.pdf.

7 Conclusion

PLANNING FOR COASTAL RESILIENCE

The Sundarbans is the world's largest remaining contiguous mangrove forest and a wetland of international importance, spanning large portions of coastal Bangladesh and India. This transboundary region is also home to some of South Asia's poorest and most vulnerable communities. Climate change is a major threat to the Sundarbans and the forest-dependent livelihoods of its surrounding inhabitants. Yet technical information on how climate change impacts the Sundarbans' vital ecosystems and local populations has been scarce. To build a knowledge base for sound climate change adaptation and resilience responses, the analytical program presented in this book undertook numerous multidisciplinary technical studies to assess the climate vulnerability of human populations and ecosystems across the Sundarbans landscape. Critical problems addressed by these studies included inundation from sea-level rise and cyclone-induced storm surges and salinization of water and soil. The findings highlighted that the impacts of sea-level rise, when measured in magnitude and time-phasing, would differ significantly across the Sundarbans, leading to differential pressures across the political border for adaptation responses to the same environmental conditions. The salinization studies also highlighted the implications for the quantity and quality of water resources that are critical for women's and children's health and nutrition. Conservation of the Sundarbans is mandated under international conventions and treaties. It is expected that lessons from this analytical program's complex, "out-of-the-box" research approach—its multidisciplinary studies, cross-border research collaboration, and learning from regional and historical perspectives—will be useful for management of this iconic landscape.

The sea level is rising, and this trend will continue beyond 2100 even if greenhouse gas (GHG) emissions are stabilized today (Church et al. 2013). Recently published scientific reports suggest that sea level may rise by 1 m or more in the 21st century. In a changing climate, progressive salinization and inundation from sea-level rise will put densely populated, low-elevation coastal zones throughout the world at risk. Families in the Sundarbans region are already on the front line of this change. Their experience, behavior, and adaptation signal future decisions by hundreds of millions of families that will face similar threats by 2100. The research presented in this book lays the technical foundation for developing a better understanding of the changes the Sundarbans is facing, including the responses of the ecosystem and human communities. Beyond the Sundarbans region, the methodologies and findings of these studies are of interest to island nations and countries worldwide that feature high-density populations and economic activity in low-lying coastal regions vulnerable to sea-level rise.

LAYING THE FOUNDATION FOR FUTURE RESEARCH

Climate change threatens to undermine poverty-alleviation efforts in many poor countries. The threat is particularly acute in low-lying coastal areas where poor households will confront sea-level rise, the accompanying salinization of soil and water resources, and accelerated intensification of weather shocks. In response, governments and their development partners are promoting the reduction of GHG emissions, infrastructure adaptation, and stronger social safety nets. However, as related work on disaster-risk-mitigation policies has shown, social safety nets are unavoidably double-edged in climate-threatened coastal areas. Reflexive compensation for progressive salinization, inundation, and weather catastrophes will alleviate near-term suffering for poor coastal households. But it may also increase the likelihood of tragic losses in the long term—for two main reasons. First, it will encourage poor households to remain and invest in high-hazard areas that will ultimately become untenable as climate change continues. Second, inevitably rising compensation will divert scarce resources from other development objectives, threatening poverty alleviation in noncoastal areas. Ultimately, the strain on public resources may prove insupportable, leading to abrupt termination of

> "Bangladesh and India should jointly take on projects in the Sundarbans to better understand the many interconnected vulnerabilities facing this remote yet highly threatened ecosystem. Their collaborative research on occupational and physical displacement from sea-level rise will provide the key perspective on prospects for human development in the region. To facilitate informed decision-making, think tanks and other organizations should be encouraged to produce policy briefs and other writings based on research results in the Sundarbans. A common repository for published peer-reviewed studies and information on ongoing research from both countries will foster further collaboration. The joint research of the South Asia Water Initiative is a bold first step, and we must build on its momentum."
>
> —Uttam Sinha, fellow, Manohar Parrikar Institute for Defence Studies and Analyses, government of India; managing editor, *Strategic Analysis*; and distinguished fellow, Institute for National Security Studies Sri Lanka

compensation for many payment-dependent coastal households, rapid impoverishment, and forced relocation.

While the potential policy problem is clear, empirical research is needed to assess the magnitude, timing, and implications of household responses. Building on the findings of the studies presented in this book, new research can be designed to investigate the consequences of a natural policy experiment that has occurred in the Sundarbans coastal regions of Bangladesh and India. This area is among the world's most disaster-prone, with recurrent historical inundation and destruction from cyclone strikes, accompanied more recently by progressive salinization as freshwater flows have changed and the sea level has risen. The neighboring coastal regions of the two countries share quite similar topography, vegetation, hydrology, and economic potential, and both have been similarly affected by these natural events. However, their policy responses have differed considerably. As part of its social safety net, India has provided direct compensation to the affected coastal households. In contrast, Bangladesh has taken a more laissez-faire policy approach: Coastal households have largely been left to fend for themselves. New research will be designed to assess the impacts of these comparative policy approaches on short- and long-term spatial population dynamics and household welfare outcomes as functions of climate-related shocks and compensation policies. The results will then be used to assess the policy and welfare implications for the Bangladesh-India coastal region, as well as similar coastal regions in other countries.

REFERENCE

Church, J. A., P. U. Clark, A. Cazenave, J. M. Gregory, S. Jevrejeva, A. Levermann, M. A. Merrifield, G. A. Milne, R. S. Nerem, P. D. Nunn, A. J. Payne, W. T. Pfeffer, D. Stammer, and A. S. Unnikrishnan. 2013. "Sea Level Change." In *Climate Change 2013: The Physical Science Basis*. Contribution of Working Group I to the Fifth Assessment Report of the Intergovernmental Panel on Climate Change, edited by T. F. Stocker, D. Qin, G.-K. Plattner, M. Tignor, S. K. Allen, J. Boschung, A. Nauels, Y. Xia, V. Bex, and P. M. Midgley. New York: Cambridge University Press for IPCC.

List of Experts

Experts from Bangladesh engaged in the technical studies

Sharifuzzaman Choudhury (engineer)

Md. Raqubul Hasib, specialist, Coast, Port and Estuary Management Division, Institute of Water Modelling (hydrologist and GIS specialist)

Mainul Huq, CEO, Development Policy Group (economist)

Md. Saiful Islam, specialist, Coast, Port and Estuary Management Division, Institute of Water Modelling (hydrologist and GIS specialist)

Zahirul Huque Khan, director, Coast, Port and Estuary Management Division, Institute of Water Modelling (hydrologist)

Md. Golam Mustafa, scientist, WorldFish-South Asia (fisheries expert)

Md. Istiak Sobhan, environmental specialist, World Bank (ecologist)

Experts from India engaged in the technical studies

Sumana Bandyopadhyay, professor, Department of Geography, University of Calcutta (geographer)

Sunando Bandyopadhyay, professor, Department of Geography, University of Calcutta (geomorphologist)

Ajanta Dey, joint secretary and program director, Nature Environment and Wildlife Society (sociologist)

Santadas Ghosh, associate professor, Department of Economics and Politics, Visva-Bharati University (economist)

Bansari Guha, assistant professor, Sivanath Sastri College (social scientist)

Nabendu Sekhar Kar, assistant professor, Department of Geography, Shahid Matangini Hazra Government College for Women, India (geomorphologist)

Chinmoyee Mallik, assistant professor, Department of Rural Studies, West Bengal State University (geographer)

Nivedita Moitra (public relations specialist)

Anirban Mukhopadhyay, senior research fellow, School of Oceanographic Studies, Jadavpur University (remote sensing specialist)

Utpal Roy, associate professor, Department of Geography, University of Calcutta (geographer)

International consultants
Siobhan Murray, technical specialist, World Bank (GIS specialist)
David Wheeler, senior fellow, World Resources Institute (econometrician)
Norma Adams (editor)
Mary Means (graphic designer)